INSIDE *the* BUSINESS *of* GRAPHIC DESIGN

60 Leaders Share Their Secrets of Success

CATHARINE FISHEL

ALLWORTH PRESS
NEW YORK

08 07 06 05 04 03   5 4 3 2 1

Published by Allworth Press
An imprint of Allworth Communications
10 East 23rd Street, New York, NY 10010

Cover and interior page design by Leah Lococo Ltd.

Page composition/typography by Integra Software Services Pvt Ltd, Pondicherry, India

ISBN: 1-58115-257-4

Library of Congress Cataloging-in-Publication Data
Fishel, Catharine M.
Inside the business of graphic design : 60 leaders share their secrets of success / by Catharine Fishel.
     p. cm.
Includes bibliographical references and index.
  ISBN 1-58115-257-4
  1. Graphic arts--Vocational guidance. 2. Commercial art—Vocational guidance. I. Title.
NC1001 .F56 2003
741.6'023'73--dc21
                              2002152007

Printed in Canada

CONTENTS

DEDICATION

For John David Reed, journalism school department head extraordinaire, who paid me for freelance paste-up jobs with back issues of *PRINT* and *U&lc*, more dear to a then-subscriptionless college student than money, and who showed me—perhaps inadvertently—that graphic design is an avocation and vocation like no other.

INTRODUCTION

This book is a tribute to the worst art director/design firm owner I have ever known.

In fact, an early working title for the book was "How Not to Be Joe" (name changed here to protect his employees). Most days, the only thing more dour than his face were the faces of his designers. Each morning, he doled out just enough rope for them to hang themselves, and by closing time, he was criticizing them under his breath for not even doing that to his satisfaction.

Since he was usually the only one to attend client presentations, only he had the information that was really needed to get any project done right. This information he meted out in incomplete spoonfuls, and when the work didn't stand up—which in his eyes, it never did—he didn't even have the courtesy to discuss the matter directly with his staff. Instead, he would stay after hours and actually alter their files.

Is he still in business? Yep. Is business good? Surprisingly, yes. Are he or his designers happy? Of course not.

Obviously, Joe is an extreme case. But he's not an anomaly: When a person has to wear creative and business hats at the same time, it's tough. For some people, it's impossible. The right- and left-brains jockey for supremacy. Conflicts, both personal and interpersonal, are inevitable. This doesn't mean, though, that life must be a misery.

In the twenty years I have interviewed and written about graphic designers, these common traits have emerged, and clearly:

1. The best designers are also the best businesspeople

2. Most designers hate being businesspeople

Another fact: Almost to the last person, the sixty-plus individuals interviewed for this book uttered some version of this statement: "We just want to have a bit of fun doing interesting work for interesting clients."

Is that too much to ask?

The firms and individuals who share their ideas in the chapters that follow don't think so. They do have fun. They do create interesting, even groundbreaking work. They consistently work with interesting clients.

So why do they succeed where Joe fails? I believe it's because they look at the business aspects of their offices with the same creative eye that they apply to actual projects. Rather than struggle through the portions of the work most readily admit they don't enjoy, they find new solutions that allow them to do more of what they truly love—design.

That's why I believed a book on the practical and creative business techniques of graphic designers would be so valuable. Because they must constantly use both sides of their brains to stay afloat, in my eyes at least, the most successful designers are really exceptional people.

So I contacted the people you will read about on the following pages. I asked them very difficult questions in some cases—personal questions about their own successes and failures—never dreaming that they would be as forthright and honest as they were. But all of them were straightforward. They told me what they had done wrong. They told me what they had done right. I was touched by the personal aspects of their lives they were willing to share in order to help another designer succeed.

Deep thanks to all of the individuals and firms interviewed for this project. You proved another axiom in which I have long believed: Graphic designers are generous to a fault.

—**Catharine Fishel**

Part One

PLANNING

Section 1: Setting Goals Is Easy— Finding Them Later Is the Hard Part

Knowing Where You Are Going

As everyone knows, the main problem with goal-setting is, at the end of the process, there are goals with which to contend. Of course, like a well-intentioned New Year's resolution, a goal can be ignored or even forgotten. Sometimes legitimate circumstances get in the way. And if the goal is a personal one, mislaying it is usually no big deal.

But when your goals involve other people, as is the case with the design firm owner, setting and meeting goals ensures everyone's survival. This section doesn't deal with setting goals—that's the easy part. Instead, four very savvy design office principals offer their advice on how, in the cold light of day, to actually achieve the goals you set.

MIRIELLO GRAFICO
Managing Employee Expectations

In the past five years, Miriello Grafico, San Diego, has undergone an evolution in the way it does business. Always very concerned with the office's creative goals, Ron Miriello and his staff are now equally attentive to its financial goals.

For Miriello, this meant being more forthcoming with employees as well as himself—no easy task. But with twenty years of experience behind him, he now knows that keeping everyone's expectations as close to center as possible offers the best chances for personal and professional satisfaction.

Ron Miriello is a nice guy. He wants everyone to be happy. Trouble is, as owner and manager of a company that employs, well, employees, he has discovered that it's just about impossible to keep everyone happy all of the time.

He shares the sad saga of the donuts, told to him by another business owner, as an example. This person had set the goal of getting his staff together as a team every Friday morning for a fifteen-minute pep talk and powwow. As an incentive, he would spring for donuts.

This plan worked famously until one morning, there was some grumbling about why there were never any chocolate donuts. Soon there were not enough donuts to suit everyone. The expectations for the donuts went up and up, until they actually became a point of contention.

The lesson, Miriello says, is that business owners and employees have to have shared objectives. When goals are set, they need to be clear to everyone. While the business owner's goal was to get everyone together to exchange news and ideas, the employees began to focus on the perk, which had somehow begun to cloud the issue.

Miriello could see himself in the same spot. Each year, his company holds half-day retreats off-site for the entire staff where goals are set, paths identified, and tasks assigned.

"I always used to come out of the retreats with a long laundry list of things to fix. I felt completely beat up, and I would think, how did this happen again?" he says. He began to recognize that allowing staff to comment on and therefore suggest any and all goals for the company was a Pandora's box. On one hand, he couldn't be held responsible for "fixing" everything himself; on the other, he was not the father and they the children who had to endure whatever he decided.

"I have learned to be clearer about what objectives I want and what I feel the staff is accountable for," Miriello says.

Miriello learned to coach his people better by getting a business coach for himself, a person who serves as both sounding board and police officer, holding Miriello true to his goals.

"The hardest thing a coach has to do is to get business owners like me be leaders. Most owners want to get in and do. They want to make decisions about how often to vacuum the office," the designer says. "His job is to pull my head away from my notepad and see if I am really doing my job. It's a bitch, really. He makes a lot of work for me, but I know he is keeping me on task."

The largest outgrowth resulting from having a business coach is that now Miriello's company has much more structure when it comes to setting and meeting goals. Each year, each department head in the eleven-person company frames his or her group's goals for the year. From that, budgets are set that include any new programs or marketing that is necessary. Then return-on-investment is studied to see if cash in is exceeding cash out.

A marketing plan outline is the result, and it is distributed at the company's annual retreats. Each leader explains departmental plans to the larger group, and everyone is encouraged to make comments. Then, as the year progresses, monthly managerial meetings are held to see if each group is staying on track and on time.

"Goals are mounted on a board, and every quarter we pull them out and see how we are doing," says Miriello, who in turn holds a status meeting every Monday with the entire staff to review current and upcoming work. With all of these checkpoints in place, Miriello and his staff all know exactly how the business is progressing.

When goals are met, the staff may have a party or go out to dinner and a show. Group vacations have even been discussed in good years. Miriello finds that what people like best as a reward, however, is paid time off. But rewards have to be established cautiously. In early 2002, for instance, with the economy's downturn, most perks would not be available.

"I used to make the mistake of trying to keep everyone happy when we all have to be accountable. When there aren't enough donuts, people get unhappy, no matter what the reason," he says. The owner recalls that when parking went from $500 to $1,500 per employee per year—an expense the business had previously covered—he had to take another look at the expense and caught a lot of grief, even though the cost had become unwieldy for the company.

"It's really hard to retract things like that when [employees] don't understand the bigger picture," he says.

People need to know where they are going and why they are working so hard. When everyone's goals are on paper and are understood, everyone shares in the hurt or reward of failure or success. Slackers in the group are also evident, so sharing objectives also has a self-policing aspect: Other team members are quick to note if someone isn't blocking for them.

Getting staff to take up this more structured approach to business has been a culture shift. "Some people might say, 'This is a whole new job. I was hired to do design, not watch numbers. We used to be all about getting big projects and winning awards, and now we are all about money,'" Miriello notes. "But it is my job is to make sure things are stable, and this structure helps me stay on top of things. I know where my business is at any one time. My employees do, too. This helps them get through successful and difficult times."

You can't manage a business on feelings, Miriello says. "You can't be saying, 'I think we are running out of money,' or 'I feel we should market more.' I am trying to move from the feeling place to the knowing place," he adds. "We structure our clients' jobs so carefully, planning out every aspect. Why can't we do that for ourselves? Now we are able to not only offer a great creative product, but we can also show off as a business."

SAMATAMASON

Emulating Client Successes

When Greg Samata opened his design office in 1975, fresh out of college and with no money or clients, his goal was just to stay in business. When he hired a young freelancer, Pat Gundersen—now his wife and business partner Pat Samata—six months later, he was still shooting from the hip.

But it was an amazing way to start a business, Pat Samata says: It forced them to think about everything they did before they did it. Their company has not had a formal business plan to date, but the couple, now in business with partner Dave Mason, see where they want to go. They get there by plain, old-fashioned hard work.

After some bad experiences with smaller clients in the salad days of their company, Pat and Greg Samata soon set their sites on corporate clients—more specifically, on annual reports. But the young firm was faced with the chicken and the egg question. How can you snag annual reports if you have no experience doing them? And how can you get experience if no one will give you his annual report?

They listened carefully to what clients wanted, and answered those requests in presentations with subsequent potential clients. They tried to school themselves in the ways of corporate life. They talked with CEOs and CFOs. What they learned was that no matter what business they were in, clients all have basically the same problems. They started to address those problems, and finally, in 1982, Helene Curtis gave them their first annual report job. Then the annual report jobs started to flow in.

Pat Samata defines that breakthrough as the first big achievement of a goal they had set as business partners. They realized at that point they could control the growth and direction of the business by targeting both short- and long-term goals.

The key to success, Samata says, is staying open-minded and always looking ahead. You don't necessarily have to be one step ahead of the crowd, just constantly aware of what is going on around you. Listen to clients and employees. Observe what your peers are doing. They will tell you how to get where you want to go.

People Power

The partners of SamataMason often take advantage of their ability to directly observe large, successful companies—their clients—in action. "We pick and chose what is working for them and apply it to our business on a much smaller scale," Samata explains.

For instance, when their children and the children of many of their employees were very small, they noted that some of their clients had on-site day care centers. SamataMason owned an adjacent building and outfitted an area in it as a nursery. The company could not provide caregivers, but employees could hire their own caregivers to come in on a daily basis. When employees wanted to see their kids, they had only to go next door.

Employees are also a vital source of ideas for making the company better, Pat Samata says. "They are very talented people, and we can entrust them to research areas that we need to learn about. They come back to us with their findings, and we rely on them heavily."

The rush of day-to-day business sometimes makes it difficult for the partners and employees to communicate, especially when they are considering new ideas or plans for the future. So, in their case, the partners tried to schedule regular meetings for everyone to touch base.

But they discovered—another insight gathered from observing corporate clients—that meetings are rarely time-efficient or enjoyable.

So they started hosting a day where a speaker, such as a printer or engraver, would share news about new technology. These were so successful in terms of educating staff and setting new goals that the events soon grew. The partners would take the entire staff to a resort and bring in friends like Clement Mok or Michael Vanderbyl to speak. It was a great opportunity, Samata says, for employees to get inspired and get to know each other better.

"Eventually, our events which we call SamataMason Days, got to be quite extravagant: Four years ago, we took everyone to Jamaica and stayed for three days in a private villa," Samata recalls. "We wanted to do something special for our people that would benefit us all."

The only requirement of employees was that everyone had to make a presentation that would be informative to the group. Each employee was free to choose a subject and format that allowed for as much creativity as possible.

Another year the group took a motor coach trip to Frank Lloyd Wright's Taliesin in Wisconsin, then moved on to visit Appleton Paper, a client, for a plant tour. They ended up at a resort, where everyone relaxed and shared ideas that were spawned during the trip. The firm has also traveled to Vancouver, where its second office is located, as well as to downtown Chicago for a ball game, museum tours, and an architectural tour of downtown by boat.

All of these events pay for themselves time and again, Samata says, in terms of defining all of the employees' goals and getting plans of action in place. She knows that even long-term employees can be reluctant to speak to the partners in the office about their ideas or concerns. "But when we are in a different environment, you get the information. The trips are definitely worth every penny," she says.

Partner Power

The partners also rely on each other's special talents to keep goals in sight. Pat Samata describes Greg as the big-picture person: He is always looking ahead at what they might get into next. Pat Samata says she has always countered Greg as the intuitive, detailed person. Dave Mason is more pragmatic than either of the Samatas, she notes, and approaches problems with logic and common sense. The three points of view often overlap, and there is a strong feeling of respect among the partners.

Communication is the key to keeping everything moving: The trio never assumes anything or takes the other person's role or duties for granted. They do their best talking, Samata says, when they are in an environment other than the office.

"When we go to each other's homes, are having dinner, or are just enjoying low-key time together, that's when we can address real concerns," she says.

Goal-setting and implementation are essential parts of any strong organization. Although they prefer to run a less structured business, one that gives them flexibility, Samata concludes, "We need goals to help us define where we are going and to what end."

LISKA + ASSOCIATES

Keeping the Big Picture in Sight

Like many designers, Steve Liska came from a background where the thought of creating a five-year, long-range business plan was unheard of: Art school just wasn't stressing business skills when he was in training.

But from the time he started his business, he has made business decisions through a combination of big-picture planning, a willingness to be flexible, and above all else, trusting his instincts. Goal-setting in the Liska + Associates office is more a matter of keeping the big picture in sight and not getting lost trying to map every single step along the way.

When he is trapped on an airplane, the food is bad, and he can't sleep, Steve Liska pulls out a notepad and sketches out his company's future. It's an occasion that occurs frequently: With twenty-five employees in Chicago and five more in New York City, plus clients across the country, he often finds himself in the air, making plans. New project ideas, strategies for existing projects, new ways to market the firm, changes in media, potential new business—all eventually find their ways to people within the company who will act on them.

The business is changing quickly, he knows, so he consciously spends time on a regular basis on such planning exercises, gauging how the world is affecting his twenty-two-year-old business. And the most important time to be planning for the future and change is, ironically, when life is great.

"It's actually hardest to do planning when you are busy and you think everyone loves you," Liska says. "At that point, all your energy is going toward your clients, so it's hard to stop and think about yourself."

He has been in business long enough to see great designers fail because they don't push themselves to evolve. He has watched many firms become successful, then simply go on trying to replicate their success.

"I could see firms that weren't changing, stylistically or from a business model standpoint. Principally, they were successful because they were already successful," he recalls. "But when everyone else started getting into AV and computers, more progressive firms took away their business. I always said to myself, 'Please, don't let that happen to me.'"

To avoid a similar fate, Liska operates his business through a combination of gut, instinct, sharpened through years of experience, and more formal strategic planning. But instinct always rules. This designer plays his cards close to his chest: As the owner of his office, he listens to the advice of his senior people, but he still does what he thinks is best.

Liska knows that even a comprehensive business plan won't save a business either. "It's interesting because I have seen smart people with big plans and big accounting firms who are not here anymore," he notes. Blindly following the advice of even expert advisors can be the kiss of death.

Liska admits he operates more on instinct than many would be comfortable with, but through slow growth, he is able to keep his eye on the bottom line. Not that he hasn't tried the formulas worked out by consultants that weigh out numbers of employees, the depreciation of office equipment, and so on to arrive at profit and loss figures.

"I just blur over when I look at advice like that. The bigger picture should not focus solely on profit and loss. We are all designers here:

At the end of the year, we also have to know that the work we produce was good," Liska insists. "No matter what your business plan is, you always have to do great work."

A big part of Liska + Associates' success is due to the consistent strategic process that directs its day-to-day work. Weekly staff meetings are held to examine schedules, and whenever there is a milestone change to be considered, such as the way the firm markets itself, the entire group is called in for consultation. Liska is notoriously frank with his designers on how the business is doing, and he encourages individuals to ask him questions.

But he is definitely the boss, and the goals he sets are for everyone—not any single individual—including himself. The advantage of this kind of centralized planning, he says, is the ability to stay nimble in an age where a phone call or e-mail can change the entire direction of a company.

"Great opportunities come and go in a minute. Capital expenses and unseen expenses, everything from postage to your 401K plan can be very costly," Liska says. "So you do need a plan. In fact, a formal business plan can be a good exercise to help you think through exactly what you are doing."

But be realistic: Don't slavishly chase after any goal, he says. If the plan needs to be fixed or adjusted to fit what is going on right now, take action and change it immediately. Figuring out what to do next and then actually doing it are the crucial things.

Finally, Liska recommends keeping sight of the broader rewards of working as a professional designer: You're not just a machine for making money.

"Personal goals are different for everyone," he says. "Some people think it's just cool to be in this business—that doesn't fuel me. Some people want to be big and powerful, or see how many awards they can get. When we solve a problem well and a client acknowledges it, that's what makes it worthwhile for me. When you do a good job, the money will follow."

In the end, Liska adds, owning and running a business is a very complex thing. It can and probably will take over your life. So it's important to base your business on a core philosophy and understand the real reason why you can do what you do. If you have to change or evolve, then your business can still be based on a solid foundation that will help you stay in control of its direction.

RIGSBY DESIGN

A Constant State of Becoming

When it comes to planning and goal-setting, Lana Rigsby of Rigsby Design calls herself the trail boss of her eight-person firm: Everyone in the office is involved in the completion of the trip, although she holds herself responsible for the ultimate success of the map that will get them to their desired destination.

Rigsby Design has always made getting away from the work once in a while a priority, so that the entire staff can pull back and absorb the bigger picture. But recently, the design group took an additional and very important next step.

"I'm the one who has to plan the map from Texas to Montana, down to the point where we are going to cross the river," laughs Lana Rigsby, principal of Houston-based Rigsby Design. "I don't necessarily share every decision with the staff because it can be very distracting to some. This is my job—everybody doesn't need to know everything."

Even so, she wants everyone on her staff to have a perfect appreciation of the "4,000-foot helicopter view" of the entire trip. The big-picture perspective is something she learned from Lowell Williams, now of Pentagram, whom she worked with for ten years at the start of her career. From Williams, Rigsby learned how important it is to "begin with the end in mind."

Rigsby has developed a number of planning methods. When she opened her own studio, to help maintain focus on her goals in the bustle of day-to-day business, she kept a notebook open on the edge of her desk. On it were written these three category headings: Now, Soon, and Maybe. This is where plans were funneled and organized. Today, she doesn't keep the notebook anymore, but the system still works.

"It shows me what we are doing now, what we can conceivably get, and blue-sky items. The times where we have gotten into trouble are when I am concentrating too much on one area or another. Maybe there is too much work in-house, so there is no dreaming or marketing going on," she says.

Rigsby and her staff have always paid close attention to planning. In the past, they might have gone off-site to just sit together, talk, and get away from the work. "We have a very intense office," the principal explains. "People don't necessarily walk; we are running most of the time."

In the fall of 2001, when the AIGA conference was originally canceled due to the events of 9/11, Rigsby decided to formalize the firm's get-togethers: She planned a first-ever conference just for her company, the Rigsby Design Rodeo and Vision Quest, late October of 2001. Speakers from outside the office were invited to present, and employees were asked to make presentations as well. Everyone was a roundtable participant at one time or another. Every subject discussed over the two-day event focused exclusively on the company's visions and energies.

"This was an absolutely wonderful planning tool," says Rigsby, who hopes to hold similar in-office conferences once or twice each year from now on.

The event began with a Thursday morning pre-conference huddle for the Rigsby Design team, which briefed everyone on the company's financial situation. Records from the previous three years were opened up, so employees could see the trends in business, the size and types of projects that had been done, and plenty of other "seriously confidential material," says Rigsby. "I know a lot of business planners would be terrified to do that, and frankly, I was, too. But the more knowledge people have, the greater their personal stake."

The printed agenda book states that at 8:00 A.M., day one of the conference, "Krispy Kremes arrive, the coffee starts brewing, and the group assembles for a team photo." After that cordial start, Lana herself got the ball rolling with a brief autobiography of her company. Then each employee was asked to give a five-minute autobiography of him- or herself, together with a favorite photo from anytime in that person's life; an artifact that expresses something personal; and a favorite quote or anecdote.

Session 3 invited employees to bring in five 11" x 17" digital photos that somehow expressed something important about the company's soul and character, plus an imaginary, overheard conversation in which a client described what it's like to work with Rigsby Design.

The next session asked everyone to tell a story of something each person accomplished that he or she is proud of, together with three adjectives that defined how that person saw his or her role at the company.

Sessions five and six concentrated on how to measure the company's success in the next few years and gauged the prevailing winds in the firm's immediate market and in the design field in general.

The last session of the day, which was followed by dinner and a movie, was a no-holds-barred roundtable discussion on how the company can improve. How were they shooting themselves in the collective foot? What market perceptions stymied them? How could they pull together more effectively?

On the second day, following breakfast, the crew reviewed what they learned from the first day of the conference, identified prevalent themes, and pinpointed what actions they would take next.

"What will we be doing in a year, two years, four years? Even our intern got involved in that," Rigsby says. Effective Monday, the next day of business following the conference, to-do lists of immediate action items were implemented. Follow-up sessions since the conference have assessed the progress of longer-term goals and kept the momentum going.

The entire event was meant to help Rigsby and her staff understand who they are and visualize what they could be. This type of planning is what lets them sleep easy at night. When people don't plan, Rigsby says, they have no clear intent. That's what planning is: Understanding your intention.

As the firm's conference booklet reads in part, "Rigsby Design, like the people who come together every day to comprise it, is in a constant state of *becoming*... and what we're becoming now is completely up to us."

Section 2: Reputation—Boost or Burden?

Can You Hang Yourself on the Hook You've Created for Clients to Grab Onto?

Graphic designers work very hard to become well-known by clients and peers. But once they arrive at some degree of notoriety, the view from the top isn't quite what they expected. It's easy to get pigeon-holed for a certain type or style of work, and once that rut is established, it's hard to climb out again.

In this section, you'll learn how four different firms deal with the reputations they have earned: one for the sort of work it does; one for its sheer size; one for its philosophy; and one for its style of work. Each has learned to use its hard-earned acclaim to its advantage.

CAHAN & ASSOCIATES
Putting Your Reputation to Work

In the last twelve years, Cahan & Associates has become synonymous with annual reports—strong, clear, award-winning annual reports. The firm has become expert in helping clients with difficult-to-understand products or services to make their offerings appreciated by stockholders and investors.

With its seemingly endless supply of concepts, the San Francisco–based company has truly revolutionized the field of annual report design. Of course, this could be a double-edged sword: Over the years, clients began to think that this is all Cahan does. But instead of letting its reputation—albeit an excellent one—overtake the firm, principal Bill Cahan has found ways to put it to work for him and his eighteen-person firm.

Cahan & Associates has more than 2,000 design awards to its credit, and nearly 70 percent of them are for its stellar annual report work. So it's natural for clients to believe that the best place to get their annual report done is at Cahan's offices. But they also think if they want a really innovative ad, then they would do better looking elsewhere.

In fact, many are surprised to learn that the firm had done packaging for companies like Coca-Cola, Pottery Barn, Tanqueray, Dole, Apollo Ale and Lager, and Star vodka, as well as bike catalogs and advertising for Klein (a subsidiary of Trek bicycles), and advertising for Informatica (which was leveraged from the design and strategy of the annual report they designed for Informatica). They also have done event design for Oracle, and branding work for many entities like Stroock, Stroock and Lavan, and the Deyoung Museum.

Owner Bill Cahan says that he understands clients' preconceptions. But he also works hard to defeat them. What he wants them to understand is that what his firm does best is not a specific job like annual report design, but bringing out that little nugget about a company that makes people care about it. Whether it is designing direct mail, advertising, or whatever, Cahan & Associates is always trying to capture the reader's heart and brain.

"It's about understanding the client, understanding their customers, and hitting them on an intellectual and emotional level to create a visceral response," Cahan says.

The development of a reputation for strong annual report work was inadvertent. When he first started out in business, Cahan actually did a lot more brochure work. "But I soon realized that this was not a good business plan because companies only do brochures once in a great while," the designer says. He realized that he needed a better strategy to stay in business.

He stumbled across an annual report show twelve years ago, and that's when the light went on, "I realized that the SEC required a company by law to put out an annual report or 10k and had the not-so-unobvious epiphany that a company needs an annual report each year, and it was a built-in annuity—that's when I decided that getting into the annual report business made good business sense."

He also realized that, at the time, the market for the annual report was extremely conservative and was underutilizing its potential. Cahan saw an opportunity to leverage the thinking his firm did on the annual report into other areas, such as advertising, public relations, sales and marketing, and recruitment.

The firm's niche soon developed. At that time, there were not many firms who specialized in this type of work, and many clients simply were not allowing even the most talented agencies to do especially innovative work for them. Cahan began to push the boundaries of the category outward in terms of design, production, and printing. Clients and designers alike took notice, and notoriety soon followed.

Having a specialty has its pluses and minuses. Cahan says that if a firm does everything equally well, then it should probably do everything. But opportunities open faster when there is a niche for clients to grab on to. On the downside, particularly with annual report work, when budgets get cut, one's specialty can be at great risk. In addition, a design staff can become very bored with doing only one sort of work day after day.

So today, Cahan and his staff are working hard to educate their existing clients about their other capabilities.

"I have always known that we needed to diversify from a purely creative standpoint, if for nothing else, just to keep our lives interesting. But now, with so many good design firms out there, it is harder for us to differentiate ourselves. So we have to keep looking for more and different opportunities," he says.

For Cahan and his staff, smart thinking is their mantra and differentiator. That means being able to unravel complicated technologies and being able to express them in emotive and digestible ways. It also means operating on a business level equal to that of their clients.

"I don't think that many designers like business or like to talk to a CFO or CEO because what they do might seem boring or difficult to understand," Cahan says. "But the more you look at clients, the more interesting they become and the better work we do. We talk to them strategically and appeal to their business side when we talk about design, and then we are able to get to that nugget that makes them unique."

As a result, Cahan has been able to attract clients from other disciplines. A case in point is Coca-Cola, Inc., whose representatives had seen an annual report Cahan and his designers had done for Adaptec, a company that had low visibility because it was so poorly understood by many people in the financial community. The design firm's work made sense of Adaptec's PCMCIA (Personal Computer Memory Card International Association) peripherals and how critical they were to the PC marketplace, garnering Adaptec the visibility it needed. (The project also landed Cahan on CNBC and CNNfn.)

Coke saw what Cahan was able to do for a high tech company and wanted the same thing for its organization. "They were able to see that our thinking could be applied to other areas of business," the principal says. "That is how we can make doors open."

One other pitfall of being known as the top dog in any field is that clients may believe that one's prices are commensurate.

"The kiss of death is getting a reputation for being too expensive, which is simply not the case with us," Cahan says, adding that his firm is absolutely not the priciest one out there and that they do continue to negotiate. Money is really the least important part of the equation, as far as he is concerned.

What is most important to Cahan are clients who understand and appreciate the benefit of his firm's strategic thinking and who value the entire design process. "We look for clients who respect what we bring to the table, and at the same time want our clients to be engaged—the work we do is about them, not us."

In the recent economic downturn, Cahan has become even more client-centric then ever. He is vigilant about coming in under budget for his clients, knowing that it is a difficult year for them. In addition, his firm has kept clients who have little money right now to spend on collateral or an annual report.

"You don't abandon people just because they are having difficult times," Cahan says.

LANDOR ASSOCIATES

How to Defeat Complacency

What is the power of the Landor Associates' brand? Ninety percent of its business comes over the transom or by referral. All twenty of its offices, in sixteen countries, are inbound marketing-based. When client development managers pick up the phone, they are almost always responding to a client query, not hustling to make a sale.

The danger of this success, of course, is creeping complacency. An organization can become so comfortable with its leadership position that it forgets how to be competitive. In this article, Landor's dynamic chairman and CEO shares what his firm is doing to shake off the cobwebs and get re-energized.

When the phone is always ringing, it's easy to forget how to actively pursue new business. In 2001, the phones were very quiet at plenty of design firms, including Landor Associates' major U.S. offices in San Francisco, New York, and Seattle.

On the surface, such a business slowdown wouldn't seem to be a problem for this world-class firm, just a momentary blip in everyday operations. But Landor Associates chairman and CEO Clay Timon says that the event was something of a wake-up call for his company.

"We found that we were not equipped psychologically or physically to go back out and prime the pump. We had grown complacent, not stayed aggressive," he says.

The company had never had any form of an in-house client development group—people whose sole responsibility it was to constantly beat the bushes looking for new prospects. Solving this physical problem within the organization was not difficult: Timon identified people in each office and region to do just this.

That was the easy part. The more difficult task involved recalibrating the mindset of the people who work for Landor: How could the company's executives convince the staff that the organization needs to be constantly thinking about client development? And how could that message be communicated so that the employees would interpret the change as a new source of strength rather than a weakness or an ominous sign? It was a dramatic culture shift for employees who had always been accustomed to clients knocking on their door.

The staff also had to understand that client development could take one of two forms.

"The most important form and the one we are focusing on now is new business from current clients," says Timon. "Then there is new-new business, or business from new clients."

Previously, once a project was completed for Client A, Landor would then concentrate its efforts on wooing Clients B and C, rather than following the path of least resistance by building on the existing relationship with Client A, with whom it already had a relationship. But today, two-thirds of the company's business comes from existing-client relationship-derived work.

In order to transform its attitude toward client development from one of complacency to aggressive pursuit, Landor Associates started talking about the work it did in a new way. Employees abandoned the idea of calling what they did "projects" and began talking about, simply enough, "clients." If you walked into a Landor meeting today, you would hear people talking about "developing new relationships with clients," not "looking for new projects."

It is not just an issue of semantics: Everything truly goes back to the client, Timon says. Landor's longest-standing client relationships are called "KCRs" or "Key Client Relationships." There are "client relationship managers" who now report directly to top management. In addition, there is one Landor officer in charge of each relationship.

Another change at Landor involves the language its people use in meetings with clients: They have balanced the use of what might be called "designer talk"—words like "logo" and "identity"—by also talking strategically about "brands" and using the client's language. They speak holistically of how a brand will affect the client's entire business—in retail applications, in investor relations, in advertising, and more. The goal is to look at design solutions from the same perspective and with the same concerns as the client.

These shifts are focusing Landor employees on the people with whom they are working, not just on the project. This approach has had an additional benefit: It has increased Landor's ability to manage changes within its client relationships. For example, at most firms, if the client lead is taken off the account or leaves the company, the client typically undergoes some form of "transition angst." In contrast, the relationships Landor builds with its clients create a level of comfort on the client side that can counteract the challenges of potential personnel shifts, timing delays, and production difficulties.

Timon cites FedEx as an example. Over the past nine years, five different Landor client managers have maintained the company's relationship with FedEx. Despite these personnel changes, the partnership between the two companies has endured and grown.

But having such stellar, long-term clients as FedEx, P&G, Frito-Lay, BP, and Ford can also work against Landor. Sometimes prospective clients see the company's success and assume that its pricing would not fit their budgets. And when business and monies are contracting everywhere, Timon knows that an under-educated prospect—one who does not fully recognize the value Landor can add to a brand—might shy away from his company.

Losing a prospective client because of cost is a concept Timon refuses to accept. According to him, the firm has to be responsible for providing the prospective client with all of the information it needs to make an educated decision.

"If we lose a prospective client for that reason, it's because we failed to convince them that the value we bring is worth what we charge," he says.

The goal in all of these efforts is to help Landor secure a reputation for being entirely client-focused. Timon admits that even though this transformation is underway, it is probably just starting to show up on the radar screens of prospective clients. Landor must continue to work hard to become widely known as a relationship-centric firm.

Complications abound: For instance, like many growing companies, Landor is making acquisitions of new offices in different parts of the world. All of these new offices must then be educated in this approach to client development.

"As we acquire new companies, how do we integrate them into the Landor culture so that all existing clients feel comfortable with them, too? That will be the next big cultural issue we will face," Timon explains.

In a very real sense, Landor Associates is in exactly the same boat as its clients. The company must remain strategic, yet creative. It must be aggressive. It must be global, yet local and personal. It must be constantly mindful of its reputation.

"Companies are now understanding that they must look for other global firms to partner with," Timon says. Landor Associates stands ready, he adds, to be that partner.

BULL RODGER

Reputation as a Control Factor

Bull Rodger, an eighteen-year-old design firm based in London, is known for its sharp sense of wit. Clients come to the agency when they want an intelligent message, delivered graciously and cleverly. Oftentimes, clients work in rather cerebral fields: They need a design firm that can speak confidently to their customers.

But does this reputation limit the firm's circle of possible clients? Possibly, says principal Paul Rodger. And that's not necessarily a bad thing.

Paul Rodger, principal of Bull Rodger, looks at reputation this way: When he goes into a meeting with new clients, he assumes they don't know his firm from a hole in the ground. Bull Rodger may have a reputation for an admirable sort of savvy work, but each new job is a chance to prove itself anew.

The firm is not a vertical specialist—that is, it doesn't focus on just annual reports or advertising, for instance. It does not have a recognizable style. It doesn't even focus on working with one particular category of clients (although the bulk of its work is business-to-business, a niche that has developed by circumstance and not design).

"We work in a very conceptual space. We do campaigns that work across a lot of media—one big idea that works everywhere for a client—literature, press ads, merchandising, Web sites. Across everything, there is continuity, the one good idea," Rodger explains. "Selling that sort of catholic attitude guarantees that we don't get pigeon-holed."

If clients call his firm for anything specific, it is for a certain attitude—a smart, witty attitude. But Rodger never wants a client to look at a past job and say, "Give me something just like that." That is allowing clients to steer his business.

Playing to one's long suit is fine, he says. In fact, his office is currently doing a lot of work with large law firms. "We have a lot of experience with law firms. It makes sense to see how many more we can get. We understand their market. But it would be awful if that was all we did and we became the law-firm-design-firm of choice," Rodger says.

There is a real danger, he says, in allowing clients to define what a design firm is, no matter how much business it brings to the door. He cites the example of designer David Davis, whose firm, DDA, opened its doors in 1985, the same year Bull Rodger opened.

"He was very style based and driven. There was almost nothing he would turn down. Five years later, we had four employees and he had a hundred. The problem in getting big that quickly was that it became a huge sausage machine. The firm was immensely popular for a while, but it was all a bit thin," Rodger says. "They became one of the early crashes in the 1990s."

By comparison, Rodger points out The Partners, also based in London, which he sees as securely founded on strong, conceptual work. "Ideas don't go out of fashion," he says. "They consistently win more awards than anyone else in this country."

Because it has confidence that it is also doing good work, Bull Rodger uses its reputation in another way: It is very particular about the clients with whom it will work.

"We need quite bright clients, I think," Rodger says. "It takes a strong client to let us do what we want to do. They are bright people who get the joke. They will always pick the cleverest ideas. If we give clients a range of solutions from safe to having turned the risk button way up, I find that, surprisingly, our clients—even law firms—will go for something a bit riskier."

Bull Rodger clients also have to accept the fact that the firm is small—only seven people—and will stay so. They have not aggressively expanded because they didn't want to. First of all, a large firm causes people to get bogged down in matters they don't want to deal with, says Rodger. In addition, the firm's principals want their customers to have direct access to the people doing the real work, not just to account managers.

"This comes from when I had to work with some real crap suits when I was a lad getting started in small agencies. Some liaisons with account managers are wonderful, but they are as rare as hen's teeth, in my experience," Rodger says.

Their office's physical space is small, too—about one thousand square feet that can be taken in in about twenty seconds. Clients like its homeiness. "We work as more of a team here—ideas come quicker that way, and we get more robust ideas working like this," the principal says.

Even the firm's self-promotions are kept in check: Only about five hundred lucky people are on what Rodger's calls "a fiercely self-indulgent" promotional mailer list. Through experience, the designers have learned that while many people will pay lip service to their sense of wit, most just want to play it safe and do what everyone else is doing. These people will never get a mailer from Bull Rodger.

Reputation is a double-edged sword, Rodger says. You do the work you like and promote yourself accordingly, but you have to hope there are enough people out there to support your habits. "Only clients who share our point of view will want to work with us," he adds. "It is very self-limiting—we are never going to be a Wolff Olins."

But, he adds, anyone who wants to build a successful firm has to do it by being passionate about what he is doing. Success does not come from mindless repeat performances for clients: Eventually, the thrill will be gone for everyone involved.

MICHAEL SCHWAB STUDIO
Sticking with a Good Thing

Michael Schwab has always loved figurative drawing and the unique interplay of positive and negative space he builds into his illustration and graphic design work. He has a highly recognizable style—dramatic, heroic, and very American.

But having practiced this manner of working for thirty years, he has to face two dilemmas regarding his professional reputation: First, how can he keep the style of drawing he loves fresh in the eyes of art directors? And second, how does he deal with imitators who admire his track record and therefore emulate his art, although not nearly as competently? The artist is not discouraged in the least.

Michael Schwab is actually rather pleased that there are artists out there who want to copy his work. Part of his satisfaction comes from the imitation-as-flattery principal. Part of it comes from the fact that he is contributing to less experienced artists' learning processes: When he was a fledgling artist, he borrowed heavily from his own heroes, including European poster artists Holwein and Bernhard. Copying is how artists train their hands and eyes, Schwab says.

But perhaps the main reason the artist does not fear imitators is that they inadvertently promote his work.

"My art is apparently hard to duplicate. The fact that art directors can't go to someone else and quickly get art with the same integrity and style that I offer has kept me afloat," Schwab says. His excellent reputation is built not on the style of his art, but on the superior level of communication it provides.

Staying Inspired

"I love what I am doing," Schwab says. "I look forward to the next day when I can be back working on my table. I love it like an actor loves the stage."

The artist says he is rarely intimidated by the reputation that precedes him, a reputation proven by dozens and dozens of awards and special recognition, including the American Institute of Graphic Arts Environmental Leadership Award, special recognition from publications such as *Communication* Arts, and the release of a new book, *The Graphic Art of Michael Schwab* (Graphis). He truly enjoys creating imagery that is powerful and dramatic—but it never, ever starts that way. It doesn't come easily, he says.

"I love to work, but lately, there are times that I wish I had more time to actually sit at my drawing table and draw instead of pacing in front of my computer negotiating fees back and forth and hearing about potential projects, interviews, and so on. However, I'm always worried that, starting tomorrow, the phone might not ever ring again," he says.

Schwab believes that the best way to maintain an excellent reputation among his peers and clients as well as to stay vital in his own mind is not to be trendy. It's the surest path to becoming stale, he says.

"It is so tempting for an artist to go in a direction, whatever it is, that is trendy—it is exciting. But I have to be careful to create what no one else is at the time. I don't see my work as merely defining an era such as the WPA or art deco either, as some detractors might. It is after those styles, but my work is always, slowly evolving," the artist notes. He will go through waves of specific subject matter—just

drawing animals, then a wave of doing, for instance, large heads—
and at this writing, he is interpreting California landscapes. Each new
trial attracts different clients; each new exploration leads him to the
next path.

This sense of forward motion began in 1972 at East Texas State
University (before he attended Art Center College of Design), where an
instructor told him that the message and communications were to be
his number one concern. The style or fashion of the art, although it
may attract the viewer's eye initially, is secondary. That's why, when a
peer sends him a clipping of an imitator's work with a note that reads,
"Can you believe this guy?!" he doesn't get upset about the mimicry.

"It is a thorn, of course, but I don't worry about it. Imitators can't
do what I do," Schwab says. "I just hope that, for their own sakes, they
are in the process of creating their own look. When I was young, I stole
with both hands while I was learning."

The one thing that does discourage him about imitators is that
they usually are not offering any kind of communication value. There is
so much work out there that is just trying to be loud, and in all the
bright colors and swirling type, the message is lost. It cheapens the art
and cheats the reader.

"I figure I have about two seconds of the viewers' time before
they turn away. I want my art to make it easy for them to get the message. I want to communicate with them quickly and succinctly,"
Schwab says.

Other Perks

Having a solid, long-standing reputation is also beneficial to an artist
from several other standpoints, according to Schwab. First of all, he
feels that clients listen to his advice more now than they did even ten
years ago. "They really listen to what I suggest," he says, "instead of
trying to change what I do."

This level of trust is reciprocal. "I am privileged to have worked with art directors who have improved what I do. I'm like an actor whose performance is much better when pushed by a great director."

Schwab has also learned to trust himself. He explains: "In your early days, you suffer and labor so much about concepts and images. I think it's like doing physical exercise. When you first start out, it's painful and exhausting, but then you get into shape. Now the ideas come more casually, more easily. My work is better when I'm more casual—more confident."

Over time, you learn to trust yourself and your first instincts. It's a matter of following the things you love to do. That—in a nutshell—is key to the success for any kind of artist. Trust yourself and follow your passion.

Of course, that means you should be your own best self-promoter. We are all taught by our parents, he says, not to brag about ourselves: It isn't polite. But sell yourself you must, to fellow artists, to clients, to reps, to your employees. You are the product of what you do, so you can't afford to be discreet and modest, or else you'll never advance in your career. A good reputation is the end result of talent combined with confidence and a bit of patience.

"To do what we do, there has to be a healthy blend of creativity, integrity, bravery, and just a pinch of salesmanship," he says.

Part Two:
MANAGING

Section 3: Running a Business That Doesn't Eat Your Creativity for Lunch

Staying Sharp Creatively and Administratively

A strong, vital business is the goal of any design firm principal. But a thriving business can sometime start to sap a designer's energies—particularly if that person is not especially fond of administrative duties. After all, why did we get into this business: to research the relative merits of dental insurance plans or create great design?

The four firms featured in this section have each found unique ways to be good administrators and good designers. One side of their work doesn't take away from the other. Finding one's balance is the key.

GEE + CHUNG DESIGN
Listening to One's Heart

In Earl Gee and Fani Chung's perfect world, running a design studio—in their case, twelve-year-old, award-winning, San Francisco–based Gee + Chung Design—would have no business aspects at all. Of course, deal with business they must. So they handle those aspects as efficiently as possible so that they can do more of what they want to do—design.

Gee + Chung Design is one of those unique firms that have found ways to stay consistently sharp creatively and administratively. Its principals' methodologies could be called simple common sense. But what makes it all work is that, unlike so many other harried business owners, they really do listen to their hearts.

Earl Gee tells the story of a trophy client for which his and Fani Chung's team performed miracles. This was an extremely reputable client, with generous budgets and a strong record of corporate design.

So when the client approached Gee + Chung Design and asked if its creative team could produce a twenty-eight-page book in just three weeks, they said, "Yes, we can do that." The project was thick with technology, all of which had to be made approachable and human. It required the assistance of seven different illustrators and photographers, and content was developed on the fly.

"We were working day and night. Designers were laying on the floor taking naps at 2:00 A.M.," Gee recalls. "We got it done on time, and we were very proud of the result. We were rewarded handsomely. And the client was very appreciative."

On all fronts, the project seemed to be a smashing success. But the firm's principals decided that they would prefer to avoid that kind of project. "You can get a reputation for performing miracles. You and your staff can only take so much of that," Gee says.

Earl Gee and Fani Chung both have extremely calm demeanors that speak volumes about how they stay sane in an insane business. Much of their philosophy on being happy as businesspeople and as creatives springs from their upbringings. They believe in staying healthy, eating well, and getting enough sleep—not exactly earth-shattering stuff, but it's the kind of common sense that people in a big hurry usually forget.

"When we started our firm in 1990," Gee says, "we realized that to focus on creating the best design for our clients, we had to succeed in business as well. Without clients and budgets, you simply don't have the opportunity to design. Succeeding in business has allowed us to focus on design, not administration."

The partners offer ten tips that have not only kept them above water, but help them enjoy the swim as well.

1. Ready or not. When Gee was pondering whether or not he was ready to start his own business, he asked Paul Hauge, his former Graphics Department chair at Art Center College of Design, for advice. Hauge told him, "You'll know when you're ready when you're ready."

This sage, Yoda-like guidance was true to the core, Gee says. He realized he not only had to master designing and producing a job, but also selling, estimating, and invoicing the job as well.

2. A division of labor. If you are fortunate enough to have a partner, the duo says, dividing up business duties can allow both partners to focus on design as much as possible. For instance, Gee is responsible for sales, while Chung is responsible for finances.

3. The business instinct. Chung's father ran a highly successful restaurant in Hong Kong, which employed more than a hundred people and gathered accolades from publications such as the *Wall Street Journal* and *Time* for its twenty variations of squab. When she was young, her father would talk to her about the relationship between the base price of squab, the proper markup needed to turn a profit, the competition, and economic conditions.

A design business is no different, Gee says. There are fixed costs such as overhead, equipment, and materials that must be covered, while labor, competition, and the economy are intangibles. If you do a good job, you get repeat business. Chung grew up around business, so she has a strong business instinct and a knack for pricing her firm's services.

4. Good money for great work. The most important thing a designer can do to stay sharp creatively, Chung and Gee believe, is to learn to charge enough to enable yourself to do your best work. This allows you to have the proper amount of time to really understand a project and create a unique solution.

This strategy also enables you to avoid taking on certain types of projects just to meet overhead. And the better the work you do, the better clients you will get and the better budgets you will receive.

5. Sometimes it's not about money. The company's first identity project was for a great client, Sun Microsystems, but it had a very limited budget of $800. Still, the project received more than twenty awards and led to many other successful identity projects over the years for which they were well compensated.

"By doing good work, you are investing in your future, earning a 'deferred' payment of clients to come," says Gee.

6. Have you eaten yet? Westerners often greet each other by asking, "How are you?" Chinese people greet each other by asking, "Have you eaten yet?" It is imperative to keep themselves and and their staff well fed in order to stay sharp and to do their best work.

7. Sleep on it. It might sound obvious, but it is amazing, Gee says, what one can accomplish when a problem is viewed fresh in the morning. It can be very helpful to finish a presentation, for instance, a day ahead of time to allow yourself to view it with fresh eyes the next morning, as the client will.

8. Why rent when you can own? The partners say that buying their own space several years ago was one of smartest things they ever did to stay focused on design. During San Francisco's dot.com boom, some of their colleagues were forced out their spaces because of the high rent.

"Owning your own space is an investment that can grow, where renting is an expense which is unrecoverable. When you retire, you can either sell the space, rent it out, or start a new business—perhaps a coffee house for retired designers," jokes Gee.

9. See the world. Travelling is truly one of the best ways to stay sharp creatively, Chung and Gee believe. Observing different cultures teaches one to look at a creative problem from a totally different perspective.

10. Never be satisfied. The only way to grow creatively and administratively is to stay committed to learning.

A good designer is constantly looking for new ways to do things, to never repeat him- or herself. Chung's professor at Yale, Paul Rand, viewed the designer as being in a constant, difficult, uphill position: He or she must keep moving in order to go forward. The partners believe in this tenet, that there is always room for improvement.

The one thing that Gee + Chung will never do is accept any amount of money for a boring project or a boring client. A good relationship with a client, interesting work, and adequate compensation are the firm's priorities.

"That's one of the best things about staying small," says Gee. "You don't have to keep feeding this giant machine to keep it running. If you are doing things that you enjoy and that make life better, that's about all we can ask from ourselves. September 11 gave us a serious dose of reality. It made us all ask, 'How can we be more useful, relate to others better, and make the world better through what we do?'"

The most important business lesson Chung learned from her father was his strong belief in treating people with respect, whether they are customers, employees, or vendors. To Gee + Chung Design, a successful business is all about the people you work with. Good relationships allow you to work well together as a team, to do great work for your clients, and have fun doing it.

MIRKO ILIĆ CORP

Uncompromising Creative Ideals

Mirko Ilić has his limits. He has been known to yell in meetings. He fires clients. He will even send a client directly to another design firm if he is unhappy with the way a project is progressing.

It's extremely bad for cash flow, he is the first to admit. But holding tight to his creative ideals is how he keeps the business from eating his spirit alive.

Uncompromising. In a word, that's Mirko Ilić. And if he weren't so smart, witty, profane, well informed, and dead on so often, he probably would have been drummed out of business years ago. But he continues to issue work that earns gut reactions not only from clients, peers, and show judges, but sometimes, even from himself.

His reputation for being a bad boy is not good for business. There are moments when he truly wonders how his office and creativity will both survive. However, "There are many different clients in the world. All I have is my creativity. How can I explain bad work in my portfolio?" he asks.

In addition, his ultimate responsibility is to consumers, he believes, not to clients. Uncompromising behavior is for the protection of the people who will actually see and use the design. He wants to give jobs and clients the maximum without cheating or lying to the public.

Ilić does want to do the job right and tries to work with people to do that. But, "In order for me to accept work, one of three things must be there—lots of time, lots of freedom, or lots of money. One must be there; two is incredible. Three is from the dream world," he says.

He does not mean to imply that other designers who may have to compromise more than he does aren't doing good work. Sometimes the rent is due tomorrow. Other days, a big check will arrive. The degree of compromise will always be different for different people.

"But if you compromise and you do a bad job, it will be your fault. They won't give you another job anyway," he notes.

On Money

Ilić believes that if someone is a good designer, he or she better also be a good business person or manager. Clients often take advantage of the emotional investment a good graphic designer pours into his or her work. "They know we are sentimental toward the work, so they will try to get you to work cheap. They can emotionally blackmail you, knowing that if you care, you will spend many more hours than they will ever pay you just to get the work published," he says.

Sentimentality is an obstacle to making money. Clients can't control a designer's creativity—it can't be put into statistical, quantifiable form— so their unit of measure is the designer's quote. The designer may offer a legitimate quote, then shoot himself in the foot by spending far too much time on the project. But that's not always a bad thing, Ilić explains.

"If I succeed in a few percent of my projects, I feel really great," he says. "Success takes time."

On Time

Managing time—specifically, time away from his office—is a constant headache for Ilić. With just himself and two other designers on staff, he desperately wants his firm to stay small, but that means he often finds himself frustrated, doing things like sitting in meetings and creating self-promotions.

"You make money off of hours, of course. Say each employee brings in $20 per hour. If you hired 100 workers, you would be making

$2,000 an hour," he points out. "But in no time, you are turning into your father's generation, hiring and firing and having more and more computers and toys. Then other people are doing what I want to do, and I am sitting in meetings." He got into this business to be creative, not to perform mundane or mechanical tasks.

Another option is to hire a business manager or agent to go out and sell work. But the problem with that scenario is to find someone who believes in you more than you believe in yourself, he says. If you don't find just the right person—and the search may take you away from designing for hours and hours—that individual will soon be happily bringing you jobs that you don't like.

So he continues to do his own promotion and selling, and he keeps meeting hours down with one simple technique: He charges clients for time spent in meetings.

"Put it in their contract," he says. "You can give them some free hours, but then that's that. If a project doesn't work out, there are still some billable hours for you."

On Freedom

Being offered creative freedom by a client is one of the most inspirational things that can happen to a designer. Without it, he says, creativity is actually an obstacle. If you really insist on sticking to ideas you believe in, the client may think you are stubborn or arrogant. So securing creative license is essential to the success of a job.

The quickest way to secure creative freedom is to ask for less money, the designer says: Unless the client is compliant, there is just about no other way to get more leeway.

But creative freedom can also be awarded to oneself. To stay vital, Ilić constantly goes beyond the circle that is graphic design, whose history, he points out, is really very brief. He checks out book covers and interiors on myriad subjects wherever he goes. One of his recent treasures is an architecture book from 1971, which he found in a secondhand book store.

"The book was groundbreaking, but I had never seen any references to it before finding it in the store. It had never been mentioned in any design publications, probably because it's about architecture. Designers never wander beyond the graphic design section of a bookstore," he says.

He also watches Japanese and Spanish television programming, even though he cannot understand the languages.

"I am fascinated with the images," he explains. "You have to keep filling up your empty slate with ideas. Some you can use, and others you cannot, but you must stay curious."

On Managing

For Ilić, doing graphic design and running a company are two very different animals. Both are difficult. As a designer, it might seem logical to put forth one's best work in competitions and magazines for promotional purposes. But he knows clients don't read design publications, so this management strategy is a failure.

Promoting his office directly to clients is tough: Vice-presidents of creative and art directors within client companies seem to change daily, so he never knows exactly who should get his mailers. Also, it runs against his nature to proclaim, "I am great. You really need me." That's a problem many designers have, he says, since many are somewhat introverted.

Once he has made contact with a client, selling the services of his small office can be difficult, too. He feels they have lost a number of jobs when clients become concerned that so much rests on Ilić's shoulders. If he got sick, they say, what would happen to their account?

"If you don't have 'people' for their 'people' to call, they just say, 'Next!'" the designer says. But it is his job as manager, he adds, to convince clients that the individualized treatment they receive will result in a truly custom job, not some assembly-line project. When that happens, he and his staff can be at their best.

SAGMEISTER, INC.

Find Balance Between Work and Life

In 2000, Stefan Sagmeister took the most talked-about vacation in graphic design history. Subject of numerous magazine articles, a point-of-departure for a number of conference and meeting presentations, and no doubt at the center of many envious conversations among peers, his year-long sabbatical is emblematic of Sagmeister's healthy attitude toward work and life, design and business. There has to be balance, or the creativity simply won't come.

He compares being both a designer and a manager to cooking and then cleaning up the kitchen later. Cooking is enjoyable because it is creative, but sometimes you are just as happy to do the dishes and not have to think all that much.

Stefan Sagmeister uses a simple and sensible mathematical formula to always keep a finger on whether or not Sagmeister, Inc.'s creative output is paying the bills. He totals his yearly overhead—everything that he couldn't expect clients to pay for—and divides that number by twelve. Then he knows exactly how much he has to ring in in design fees per month.

"Of the small offices I know that have gone out of business, they did not have that number to check against," he says.

The day before this interview, Sagmeister had actually done a check on what the last three months of the new year would bring his office. The news wasn't especially good, but he knows exactly how to operate during that time.

"No more pro bono or low-paying jobs. We'll have to take on more corporate work," he says.

Small Office

Sagmeister is able to stay nimble and responsive by keeping his firm small—only himself, another designer, and an intern. This was a lesson he learned while working for Tibor Kalman at M&Co. But staying small can be tough.

"When I opened in 1993, there was a boom economy. We had ten times the number of jobs we could take on. Then I got to know a lot of really good designers who wanted to work here. I could have easily enlarged," he says. But then he would have become an administrator with no time to design. "If I wanted to become a manager, I would have gone to business school, which would have been much easier than getting into art school in Austria."

Sagmeister knows of what he speaks, having run the Leo Burnett Design Group in Hong Kong for two years. He witnessed firsthand how slowly the wheels of a large office could turn. He found that he had to come in at 6:00 A.M. every day, just to get in one hour of design time.

Another lesson from Kalman: Play Robin Hood. Sagmeister finds it easier to take on a few large clients, who pay the bills, which allows him to spend time on jobs that aren't as profitable but perhaps are highly gratifying.

Large Projects

Today, Sagmeister is careful to limit the number and size of jobs he will accept. For instance, he recalls one lucrative project offered to Sagmeister, Inc., that would have eaten up half of his studio's time for two years. He turned the job away: No client should be larger than one-quarter of an office's total business.

Projects can also be too small, and small jobs tend to get too numerous. Plus, a flurry of small jobs can eat up a surprising amount of brain power. His office has been open for eight years, but it is only up to Number 120 in the job ticket book. The hard lesson was that fifty of those jobs were done in the first year of business.

"I learned quickly that fifty small jobs are much more time consuming than ten large ones. Now, unless a job is lots of fun or really culturally inspiring, we don't take on tiny jobs," he says.

Bigger Challenges

Sagmeister's sabbatical in 2000 came about for a number of reasons. He did a workshop at Cranbrook and loved the feeling of total experimentation he found there. Ed Fella visited with his famous notebooks of ballpoint doodles, and that pushed him further.

But the biggest decision point was that he was having less and less fun. Every work day wouldn't necessarily be completely enjoyable, he knew, but with longer and longer stretches between moments he truly savored, he knew it wouldn't be long until the entire ship went down.

So he challenged himself to walk away from it all. During his year-long experiment, he did many of the things he had dreamed of doing—sitting around just thinking, experimenting with different working formats, finally checking out all of his accumulated books. The lesson that he learned, though, was probably even more valuable than the enjoyment factor: Stay off guard. Reject the familiar and embrace new challenges.

"Paula Scher is a good example of someone who does this: She has been working for thirty years, and her work is still so relevant. How does she stay excited? She switches from one thing to another. She tries things she knows very little about," he says.

This is admirable, but for Sagmeister, it is also unnerving. He worked on a music video recently—his first ever—and admits he was very scared.

"There was a catering table there, and every time I passed it, I wanted to hide under it," he says. But every project should make one's heart beat like that. Because if it doesn't, it won't make the client's pulse race either.

"Projects should be done at the level where it excites [a potential client] enough that he gives you a call," he says. "Every project that is mediocre and that you can't show in your portfolio hurts you because you will lose the chance to get another, better assignment. It's impossible to get upscale projects in your portfolio unless the client has high expectations of you."

Bigger Expectations

Sagmeister knows that there is a fine line between egotism and making sure a project gets done the right way. Gauging how amenable to be with a client was yet another lesson learned from Tibor Kalman.

"He spent most of his energy at M&Co to make sure a project got through verbatim. He would truly put everything on the line, even turn away a whole year's worth of work if things weren't going right," Sagmeister recalls.

The first time he saw this happen, it was like a light bulb going off, the designer says. "That's why M&Co was the best company around for ten years—not because they were so much smarter, as there were many others around with good intellect and similar capabilities—but because of Kalman's commitment to get it done right."

Running a design company 100 percent of the time as a manager is not interesting to Sagmeister. Being a designer all of the time doesn't intrigue him either. "I am happy doing both," he says. Balancing, he adds, is the key.

TERRY MARKS DESIGN
Seven Postulates for Good Business

Terry Marks is the first to admit that he "fell" into design, that he didn't really set out to become the principal of a relaxed and fun-loving office in Seattle. Four years into college, he finally declared his major in Communications/PR and Art. After an internship and a brief stint as an in-house designer, he found himself freelancing, and quit his day job. A decision to move to Seattle soon found him overwhelmed with work. So he started hiring people.

He loves the work. He loves the relationships he has developed with the people he has met. But he knows that it would be very easy to become overwhelmed with it all.

Terry Marks stays happy in his six-person office, Terry Marks Design, by acknowledging these seven postulates.

1. Busy is crap. In a business where everyone is always asking, "Are you busy?" Marks knows that every second of every day can be eaten up with activities that don't earn money, or improve relations with clients, or actually do anything positive. You have to be doing things that make you and the business prosper, not just "staying busy."

2. There are many jealous goddesses. So many things must be attended to. "You only get things done by putting in time at the shrine," Marks says. "It's a big balancing act. You have to focus on different things at different times in order to get what you want."

For instance, Marks' firm was one of many that was stung by the demise of the dot.coms. He knew there were significant monies that he would never see, and clients that were gone forever. "But even embracing that abject sense of failure then allows us to see what success is later," he notes.

3. Business is like dating. There has to be friction to create something good. When the magic is bled from what you do, clients start shopping elsewhere.

4. Dating is stupid. We all want something more from the experience than we will ever get.

5. The world is small. "I knew I had abilities when I got started in this business. But you really have to embrace that you can do this. Success is so close. It really is right there in front of you," Marks says.

6. Look through the other end of the telescope. The things that hit you most in the heart, the things that really inspire and carry you along often get covered up by the dervish of trying to get everything else done and make money. The little things hit you where you live. "Whatever knocks off the barnacles," he says. "That's what you really need."

7. You get by giving away. Making money is fine and necessary, but when you create time to do things with and for other people, you get so much back. These are likely the things that will matter the most when it is all said and done.

These principles have helped Marks stay sane—and recently, to survive as a small business owner in a difficult business environment in the Northwest. He has a remarkable sense of humor, as his clients already know: Self-promotions have included guitar picks, drink coasters, and action figures of him and his staff.

"Those are the kinds of things that people in my office really dig into. They let everyone breathe a little easier. I want everyone, including me, to have room to play," he says.

Marks surrounds himself with like-minded people whom he trusts, not only inside the shop but outside, too: He does side projects with filmmakers, comic book artists, animators, and others. These relationships and projects give him energy; often times, he is crafting things purely for his own enjoyment, not for profit.

In the office, he is also protective of his creative energies. For instance, he admits that there are certain, necessary business activities that sap his strength. For those chores, he employs able gatekeepers to manage the office, handle receivables and bills, and be in charge of scheduling. He watches the bottom line, but doesn't want to get involved too deeply in its day-to-day maintenance.

Marks is careful in delegating responsibility, though. "You can give people enough rope to hang themselves, or you can help build them a ladder to get where they want to go," he says. "You have to let people know that you trust them; otherwise, you will end up doing everything."

At the same time, he says, business owners can't be constantly afraid of losing control of their company just because they redistribute responsibilities. "There is too much fear in this business—fear of making business mistakes, fear of what others think. The worst thing you can do is be fearful of the opinions of the people who work for you," he points out. A firm owner simply cannot be surly, stomp his or her foot down, and proclaim that he or she is in charge, dammit.

"Letting pettiness creep in to the point where you are guarding everything is ridiculous," he adds. Instead, Marks brings in people whom he feels confident are better than he is in specific areas. "Even if these are part-time people, it is cheaper to pay others for what takes you twice as long. You could be making money instead of costing the company money."

The machine has to perpetuate itself without killing the people who support it: That is what the business owner is there to guarantee, at the very base level. If Marks is not feeling motivated, the machine will also falter. So he keeps first things first. Being able to support life and limb as a designer is fantastic, Marks says. But keeping yourself inspired along the way is what makes it all worthwhile.

"If you are not feeling fulfilled, you haven't trusted yourself, or you are not challenging yourself, or you are just too busy. If you are too busy, hire someone to help out or choose to get less done. We have gone both ways on that," he says. "Do personal projects before or after work, but you have to always be creating something enjoyable for yourself."

Some firm owners do choose to step away from the creative side of their businesses, and that's fine, Marks believes. But those people cannot then choose to also keep an iron fist over what the creatives on staff are doing. Designers need projects that belong to them; they have to have room to work. Imposing one's ego on the creative process is like dropping poison into the water barrel, he says.

"You have to be a cheerleader and a champion at the same time," Marks adds.

Section 4: You Can't Paddle If You're at the Helm

Building on the Star Quality of Your Good Name

There's a saying at Leo Burnett that there is one person's name on the door, but hundreds of people work there. A new client certainly wouldn't expect to obtain Mr. Burnett's personal attention. Instead, that client understands that the employees inside all share a core philosophy, which is essentially what attracted the client in the first place.

But for some reason, while this convention works well amongst advertising agencies, designers who decide to start a business under their own name can find themselves painted into a strange corner: Clients may love their work, but they often expect the person whose name is on the door to do the work, attend the meetings, and even answer the phone. In this chapter, four different high-profile designers offer their ideas on building on their good names and crafting a firm that can thrive even if they chose to step away from it someday.

KIKU OBATA & COMPANY
Taking Turns at the Plate

Kiku Obata is an actual person—although some people, even in the graphics field, believe that this is solely the name of a business, perhaps a moniker built from the last names of two partners. It works in Obata's favor.

This confusion allows her to step forward as the firm's figurehead in certain situations, or to stay in the background at other times and let her staff and their work represent the firm.

Clients are perceptibly charmed when greeted by Kiku Obata, the soft-spoken principal of the St. Louis–based, multidisciplinary design firm that specializes in creating and implementing identities, places, and ideas for clients by integrating graphic design, architecture, environmental graphic design, interiors, and lighting design.

"Sometimes people don't even realize that there is a 'me' behind the name," she says. The pleasant confusion cultivates intrigue, and Obata relies on her firm's reputation for exceptional design to drive the name. "That's okay. It really is best when the name comes to represent the firm and the passionate and creative team of individuals that comprise it. That helps us plan for continued success and possibly succession somewhere down the road."

Looking to the Future

Obata consciously employs a number of efforts to help keep her firm healthy and thriving in its new digs in the City's famous Loop district.

Her efforts to safeguard success for the firm's future begin with establishing effective internal systems and practices.

One such practice occurs at the beginning of each new year with the development of a strategic plan for that year. The strategic plan, developed by Obata and the firm's vice-president, Kevin Flynn, outlines the company's accomplishments during the previous year, and restates the firm's mission and shared vision of integrating creative skills to achieve design excellence, implementing best client practices, promoting continued professional development, and contributing to community.

The strategic plan sets goals and action items for the entire design, marketing, and operations team. Cross-company buy-in for the plan is then ensured during scheduled, individual reviews where employees are asked to provide feedback about the plan and to share their professional goals for the year. Knowing the company's goals helps staff members make their own educated decisions about design directions.

"We have a process set up for design reviews so that I am not the only one offering feedback. In a review, there will also be other people from the staff—an interior design person, an architect, and graphic designers. The project is looked at from all angles," Obata explains.

Team Focus

Being kept apprised of the company's goals and empowered to make decisions permits individuals at the company to work in responsive, autonomous teams. When Kiku Obata & Company promotes itself, these teams and their work draw the focus, not the company's principal. The firm has been very successful in gaining valuable exposure in industry publications and in region-specific publications highlighting recently completed projects around the country. The media buzz underscore's Kiku Obata's vitality as both a firm and a brand, and of the teams' hard work and talent.

As head of her company, Kiku Obata allows her name to be put forward in promoting civic leadership and community revitalization and enhancement. "I try to promote what our firm does for the community. After working on projects all over the country, we made a commitment two years ago to do more for the St. Louis community, through public and private projects," she says. For these projects, the company's good name is reinforced when Obata is the person the public sees at the wheel.

Together, Obata, as the company's owner, and Flynn, who manages the company's architectural projects, control the firm's growth. In the past five years, Obata learned a valuable lesson about how her company's vision for growth worked—or didn't work. "We were up to forty-five people at one point. I sat down and realized that if I wanted to spend just one hour a week with each employee, I couldn't do it anymore," she says. Through attrition, Obata allowed the firm's size to go back down to thirty. "That made a big difference in my quality of life, in the continuity of the firm, and in being able to maintain personal interaction with people."

Obata gauges that a manageable maximum of thirty-five employees will allow her firm's systems to stay in place. The staff's conservative size limits the scope and number of projects the firm can handle, but in a nice way, according to Obata. It causes her to focus on her team's core strengths, which meld architecture, interiors, lighting, environmental graphics, and graphic design.

"You have to discover your pace, and your staff's pace, and then concentrate on what they really like to do. It really is about developing and keeping exceptional talent. It's about passion and allowing the creative freedom that unlocks potential and gives rise to new possibility and new ideas. It's important to make people feel they're an integral, contributing member of a team and to let them see what can be achieved when they integrate their skills," Obata says. She does not rely on external indicators to set the course for her firm. Instead she pays close attention to the mood and talents of her staff, and responds in kind. Her guidance is more instinctual and based on her many years of experience.

While she quietly steers her firm, Obata also is keeping careful watch for what the next big area of business will be for her company. What is the next brand? How can they apply their specializations to upcoming opportunities? By assuming the role of pilot, Obata has let go of a lot of day-to-day design decisions and operational responsibilities. Kevin Flynn handles most of the project management duties and employees have been carefully trained to accept new challenges. She feels comfortable now that the business is in good hands.

"We have a great team here right now," says Obata, "with people who really step up to the plate and who understand what distinguishes us from other firms."

TRICKETT & WEBB

Lots of Small Pyramids

*When Brian Webb of Trickett & Webb, London, graduated from college
in the late 1960s, he says that design—as a business—didn't really
exist. So there wasn't really anyone to look to for guidance or
precedent. He and partner Lynn Trickett had to find their own way.*

*Having practiced their successful design firm for thirty years now,
they've learned a lot about building a business with an excellent
reputation for good work, good sense, and good humor.*

Brian Webb says that he and partner Lynn Trickett started and
built their business by instinct. "I had never met an old designer at
that point," Webb laughs. "We didn't have any clients or experience.
Our financial support was in the form of working spouses for that first
year."

But the pair did have some solid ideas in place from the start. The
first was how to name the new company: Trickett & Webb Ltd. was
basic but sensible. They believe that companies founded with esoteric
names dreamed up late at night are doomed to failure, or at least
destined to be forever looked at askance by potential clients.
"Companies that begin in bars end in bars. Our company began at
9:00 A.M. in an office," he says.

The next step was realizing what their company philosophy was.
After about a year in business and with eleven actual jobs under their
belts, a magazine reporter came to interview the partners. Did they
have a working philosophy, the reporter asked.

"We said 'Do good work for interesting people,'" Webb recalls. "That is still basically the reason we come to work. And every job that we accept like that gets us the next job."

While a public company measures its success in terms of profits, Trickett & Webb has always gauged its success by the quality of the work that it produces. Of course, since the firm handles upwards of 250 jobs per year now, the partners can no longer monitor every aspect of every project. Instead, they use a model that ensures that both quality and growth are maintained.

The best way to grow a design company with an excellent reputation is, rather than have one pyramid with a single boss at its top, to establish lots of smaller pyramids, each headed by an employee who is a good designer and who shares the philosophy of the office. A natural division of duties emerges from this model, matching specific talents with specific jobs. Lynn Trickett specializes in finances. Another designer focuses on three-dimensional work, and another's inclination is toward new technology. Allowing each person to gravitate to their personal pyramid of preference keeps everyone happy and the level of the work good.

But when it comes to dealing with clients, every designer at Trickett & Webb would describe him- or herself as an account manager as well.

"We tell clients early on that you might be dealing with any one of us. There is no middle person. In addition, there are always at least two senior level people involved with every project," Webb says. "We work as a team and have always made it clear that collectively, we all do better than when it is just one person working alone. And a good idea is a good idea—if the cleaning lady came up with it, then it is still a good idea. It's the most wonderful thing about coming into work here — the group energy is vastly greater than what we can do alone."

The design group also encourages its clients to work hard for them: They want plenty of input from the people who hire them.

"We don't want to be handed a brief and told to come back in three weeks with one solution," Webb says. "The clients know much more about their own businesses than we will ever know. What they don't necessarily know is what to say and how to say it. We are very keen to respect that knowledge and turn it into a language that other people can understand."

Trickett & Webb works best as a democracy. But this does mean that the principals necessarily must release responsibility for some issues to their staff, which can be difficult for both the manager and the employee. For example, after meeting with a client, Webb may have a very clear idea of how the design problem might be solved, but he will only give hints to the designer who is doing the work.

"You can almost hear them thinking, 'What the hell does he want?'" Webb says. Still, he works hard to guide and not steer the designer, who he hopes will eventually take ownership of, and therefore, greater pride in the job.

Hiring designers straight from college is extremely helpful in this respect, he adds. They are usually much more open to being guided, have lots of energy, and are hungry for a degree of autonomy. Trickett & Webb work does not have a "look," but some would say it is recognizable by its sense of detail: Webb says that it has more to do with how they approach a job than with how they finish it. Because his designers have never worked anywhere but at his office, they pick up this habit quickly.

Maintaining the office's good reputation has had a lot to do with slow, organic, careful growth. People aren't brought in suddenly just to handle a single large project. There are, of course, periods where the studio is faced with more work than it can handle. Then, the principals bring in freelance computer operators to input material or to continue in a style that has already been set.

Webb feels that if a studio needs to grow, it is up to the principals to make sure it grows in the right direction. Webb cites an instance that could have been a turning point for his company. In the late 1980s in the United Kingdom, there was an enormous expansion of business. Many design firms bought bigger offices and took on huge overhead. Trickett & Webb had already purchased its own offices, and suddenly, its real estate was worth more than the partners paid for it.

"It would have been very easy to get caught up in all of the excitement, sell the space, and use the money as a down payment on a larger space. But then we said, 'Wait, we are designers, not property developers,'" Webb recalls. They decided to stay put and concentrate their energies on continuing to produce excellent design.

Building a solid reputation is not something that can be engineered, Webb notes. It's more a matter of involving clients and staff in the process all along the way, whether the job is large or small. In that way, everyone is heavily invested in the success of the job, and ultimately, happy.

Ironically, some of the biggest successes the firm has had have resulted from jobs that other offices have failed with. "We're not superstitious," says Webb, "but those no-hopers are the ones that often win all of the awards. That's not something they teach you in design school. We still do good work for interesting people—again, it's how we approach a job, not necessarily how we finish it."

CHASE DESIGN GROUP

Delegation, Finally

"That Gothic designer"—it's a curse and a blessing for designer Margo Chase. Even though she has been in business since 1986, has between five to eight employees at any one time, and does plenty of work that is nowhere in the neighborhood of Gothic, she is nevertheless personally known for a certain style of work. Success with a succession of high-profile clients has clinched that.

So Chase is faced with the double challenge of widening the horizon in which she can work and be recognized as well as getting clients to understand that they can get intelligent, exciting work from everyone on her hand-picked staff at Chase Design Group in Los Angeles, not just from her. Recently, she took the bull by the horns.

Margo Chase has never had a real job.

She has been on her own since graduating from college, where she was studying to be a veterinarian. Running a successful design firm was never intentional or planned: It just happened.

"Like many designers, I didn't take business classes and I never paid much attention [to such matters]," says Chase. "I never intended to run a company. I just wanted to do great design. But the firm evolved from a freelance business, and I've probably made every possible mistake over the years."

For a long time after she started Margo Chase Design (now Chase Design Group) in 1986, she believed that the business would take care of itself. She only accepted the work she wanted and wasn't concerned with making money: If she liked the work, that was enough.

After a few years, though, she realized that she needed help. In order to hire the help she needed, she had to start paying attention to profit. She hired various consultants over the years, mostly to little effect.

"For a long time, when I grew the company, I just lost money and had to shrink again. I really wanted a larger company so that I could take on larger projects, but I couldn't figure out how to do it," Chase says.

She also confesses to having the classic problem with delegation.

"I think it's because my name is on the door," Chase says. "It's been hard to let go and allow other people to run things. For years I couldn't afford to hire good management people so I felt like I had to do it all. It's hard to grow a business when one person is responsible for everything."

A New Start

In 2001, she resolved to do better: Chase Design Group hired marketing consultant Cliff Scott of The Scott Group. The goal, explains Chase, was to help the firm grow profitably by attracting the right kinds of accounts. "We are all about good design, but it's difficult to talk about design to non-designers so that they understand the value of what we do. I'm sick of all the discussion about proprietary process and design systems. I don't believe that's how great design gets made, and I was having a hard time figuring out how to talk about what we do in a way that felt authentic."

Scott is steering the creation of new marketing materials that will address these problems. The promotions speak to what the firm believes in and how the designers think about design, not just what they do. "His background is in marketing and advertising, so any reputation I or the firm had didn't cloud his vision. He had very few preconceived ideas about how to promote design so he could come to the problem with an open mind. That is what we needed," says Chase.

Scott has also helped her hire staff. "I'm good at hiring creative people, but it was always difficult for me to hire business and administrative people because I don't know how to do their jobs." The addition of Larry Jones to head the account management group is another step in the new direction. Now a client's first contact with Chase Design Group is usually with someone other than Margo.

"I used to be the person who did new business development, and I was not great at it," she laughs. "I love design. I like to be left alone with my team to do the work, so I didn't spend enough time meeting people and having lunch."

Another addition to the staff in 2001 was James Bradley, the first-ever company president, who brings a big-picture perspective to the firm. A former client, Bradley understands what it takes to market and sell great design. In addition to landing large projects, Bradley oversees marketing, hiring, finance, and contributes to improving workflow. Chase is also happy with the quality of attention Bradley gives to internal management.

Bradley doesn't believe in taking Chase to first meetings unless there's a very good reason. "She's the star," he says. "We don't waste her time. Margo's vision is what drives this place. Every designer working on a project needs access to a piece of the project, and we make sure they get it."

Another development has been a flow chart that outlines the management of the company. Flowing from the president, who serves as the arbiter in major decisions, is Chase as creative director, Larry Jones as account director, and Chris Lowery as operations director (or, as he likes to call himself, Minister of the Environment).

Improved Growth

One of the things about being Margo Chase is that it's not hard to attract great talent. To Chase this is key, because she believes that great design comes from great designers, not from some "process."

"I'm growing into my role as creative director of a larger group pretty happily," she says. "It's like being a coach. I'll always do some hands-on work because that's how I am, but it's really fun when other people come up with great things I wouldn't have thought of. I'm really fortunate because I get that a lot."

The thing she likes best about the recent growth of the company is the reduced number of responsibilities she now has. "When you start a small business, whether it's about design or engineering or making cakes, you suddenly find you have seven jobs, and you're probably only good at one of them. That was my situation for the first few years. Now, with the confidence that great people are doing the other things better than I ever could, I'm free to really focus on the creative side. It's a great feeling."

Bradley concurs. "That's right where we want her," he smiles.

TED WRIGHT ILLUSTRATION

Let the Work Do the Talking

Freelance illustration and design isn't for the weak and meek, says artist Ted Wright. All of the freelancers he knows are high-energy people. But even the highest-energy people are burning out these days, and many never come back to the field.

Freelancers are by definition both the manager and the employee, and usually, they overwhelmingly prefer to be the person producing the work, not the poor sap who is out drumming up new business, sending out invoices, and filing the tax forms. But drum and send and file they must, says Wright, who has discovered ways to be a great boss to himself as well as an exemplary employee.

Artist Ted Wright knows that as a freelancer, he must wear many hats. He also knows that when a person is wearing an entire pile of hats, he or she might not look very good. He accepts that. Wright knows that outsiders envy what they imagine to be a carefree lifestyle—an artist working at home with no boss—but when he tells them that he must work all day on business matters, and then pick up again from 6:00 P.M. until 2:00 A.M. to do his creative work, the picture isn't quite so attractive.

Add to that fact that times are tough for freelancers—many are abandoning the field because they can't make a living—and the outlook is even less rosy. A freelancer must be an aggressive, smart businessperson, Wright says. Being a talented designer or artist is not enough to survive anymore.

A Double Life

Wright the Manager tries to make the life of Wright the Employee easier by going after work he knows his creative half will excel in. Often, he will generate samples of jobs that he thinks he can sell, for the Boy Scouts of America, the PGA, Sea Ray Yachts, and the Pro Rodeo Association. A completed sample, rendered with the subject matter of the potential client in mind, goes a long way toward helping that person visualize exactly what Wright can do for him or her.

Also in his role as promoter and manager, Wright sends out a postcard mailing of five hundred showing his work each month. He maintains a postcard template: All he has to do to create a new one is drop in a new image.

While the postcards are effective as a regular mailing—each pulls in five to ten jobs as a rule—Wright will also use them in a very targeted way in conjunction with the release of one of his higher profile jobs.

For instance, he created the art for the 2002 Byron Nelson Golf Classic in Irving, Texas. His illustration of Byron Nelson was used on a poster and all of the tournament's print collateral. Wright knew it would have a very high exposure rate in the media, so he targeted Texas art directors with his cards, sending them out one week before the tournament began.

"That pulled in six jobs before the tournament, and afterward, many more calls came in," he recalls. Timing is crucial with these promotions. "These really big exposure jobs are far and few between. So when you get one, you want to do the most with it."

When the phone is not ringing, it's time to start making a few calls yourself. Wright is surprised how reticent some freelancers are to pick up the phone and just say "hello" to current or former clients, much less make a cold call. Call and ask if you can meet for lunch or just get together for an hour, he says: Eighty percent of the time he makes a contact like this, Wright lands a job.

"The best clients are your best friends. When you build a friendship, it requires that you spend time with that person," he says. Maintaining the friendship ensures that the line of business will also be maintained. A designer friend of his has a client who sells multimillion-dollar yachts—and who has a marketing budget to match. "He told me that if he didn't play the golf and take them out to dinner or whatever at least twice a month, his business would go away."

Another easy way to get business is just by being a good listener. When clients are talking about the course of their own business, it's surprising what kinds of valuable information a freelancer can pick up. Recently, for instance, Wright learned that a client of his—an ad agency—was turning away work in a specific product category because it competed with existing accounts. Wright asked for the names of the rejected clients right away and sent a presentation of his own to them.

"The agency doesn't care because they have already shown that client the door. I have picked up a lot of clients this way," he says.

When business is really slow, Wright uses the time to produce new samples to show clients. He will take an entire day and visit all of the agencies in his area. "If you haven't seen an art director for a long time, and are just phoning and faxing, you need to have that handshake time—that's what matters most," he explains.

Managing Personnel

Wright believes that the business has come to a strange juncture, where even very talented freelancers find themselves burnt out. They become teachers, house painters, or just plain unemployed—anything but continue as a freelance designer or illustrator.

He believes the root of the problem is the same thing that makes the freelance life seem so appealing in the beginning: Many of these people work from their homes, and a house or apartment can quickly become a prison for a busy person. Wright says he refuses to live his life on the Internet and the phone: It's not healthy not to have any face-to-face contact with people.

In order to stay in business, freelancers need to be building relationships all the time. Go to parties; go to professional functions; just get out and enjoy the Earth by taking a walk. Wright walks every day for an hour, just to recharge his batteries.

As manager, he also cuts himself some slack. The artist works extremely hard from Monday through Thursday, but Friday is reserved for "play day." Sometimes it is spent developing new work, and sometimes it is spent with his three daughters. But it has come to be time he truly looks forward to and which makes his difficult schedule bearable.

In the meantime, he tries to revitalize himself constantly so that he is inspired when the phone rings with that next really great job.

"I met a French woman at the airport recently with six suitcases and five cameras—a photographer. I asked her where she was headed, and she said she had cashed in everything to go to France to become recharged. She was going to spend three months just soaking everything up," Wright recalls. "I thought that was so exciting and inspiring. Artists sometimes have to do drastic things. Some do nothing more than listen to music or watch movies. Some have to change locations. But everybody has to find their own juice."

Section 5: How Not to Art Direct Your Staff to Death

Being a Good Manager and Inspirer at the Same Time

An art or creative director can find him- or herself in some pretty curious roles at times: touchstone, parent, bad guy, cheerleader, champion. The one hat he or she is sometimes missing is that of a creative person. There's just not enough time left in the day.

The other dilemma is that of deciding whether one's office is a democracy or dictatorship. Just what constitutes being heavy-handed as opposed to being confident and strong? A variety of art direction styles follow: from sharing art direction duties with the entire staff as well as careful hiring and training, to steering designers' work by inspiring their confidence and respect. Each art director has a valuable story to tell.

WATTS DESIGN

Everyone's an Art Director

What is the definition of an effective art director? At Watts Design, South Melbourne, Australia, it should be any person on staff, from the company's principals and founders, Helen and Peter Watts, to its most recently hired designer. Everyone in the office should be helping to inspire everyone else.

That doesn't mean every project is swarming with too many cooks; instead, this philosophy promotes an honest exchange of ideas. There is always a support system in place when it is needed.

According to Peter Watts, a good art director tells people when to stop. And according to his life and business partner, Helen Watts, a good art director tells people when to go.

These approaches aren't as far apart as they might initially seem. Young designers especially, says Peter, will fiddle and fuss with a design forever. Or they might be heading down a dead-end path.

"You have to teach them to stop when they come to the right result; if you let them go too far, they get confused," he says.

Helen wants to excite her designers with the possibilities of where they might take a concept. "I feed them with information that will take them down as many avenues as possible to where the most effective solution could lay," she says.

Where these paths cross—or at least run parallel for a spell—is in how straightforward the couple is with each other and with their designers. They also expect their staff members to regularly step into the role of art director to offer guidance to each other.

"People who work here know they can be upfront," Peter says. His goal is to inspire all of his staff not to be harsh with each other, but to feel that they are able to offer honest feedback.

Helen also wants everyone at her firm to be involved at this intimate level, but her method of achieving that end is a bit different. A person becomes a good art director, she says, by allowing others to flourish, through encouragement and exploration. She wants her people to work as a team, with each person feeling ownership of each project.

The flip side of being able to give criticism is being able to take it as well. Those who are easily offended, who don't really want to hear what the client said at the presentation, or who aren't good team players don't last long at the agency. A person with a large ego is also not a good fit at Watts Design. He or she won't allow others to explore their ideas further and is likely to take credit for work that was really a group effort.

The couple is happy with how their staff helps each other and is gaining personal insights at the same time. "We have a really good atmosphere in the studio where everyone listens to everyone else's opinions," Peter says. The danger, he says, is that those who learn to be very good art directors in this way are liable to leave their office to start their own firm.

Practical Considerations

As any art director knows, a major part of the job is keeping one's eye on the clock. For a firm to be profitable, the schedule has to be met— or does it?

Peter believes that one of the biggest mistakes he can make as an art director is to pressure staff by rushing them. Better to call the client and admit you need more time than return substandard work that was hustled out without the right kind of thinking behind it.

"I tell our designers that timelines are important, but so is the quality of the work. There is no real timeline on anything. We need the time we need to get the work done right," he says. "You have to consider people's emotions. If you put too much pressure on someone to get something out, it will show."

Helen believes that it is important that a studio accommodates individual working styles. For example, some people prefer to work steadily toward a deadline, while others perform better when the pressure is on.

"It's important to have a timeline for each project. Each of our designers will work on more than one project at a time. This allows for project hold ups, research, and also important, creative juices drying up temporarily," she says. "Designers can then move on to another job, until they are ready to go back to the previous design. We make sure that clients are always kept informed of what stage their project is at."

The Watts' disparate approaches work well under the same roof. Company procedures have been put in place to ensure that, whatever the personal style of the art director, the work goes through the same quality processes.

Peter believes that a good art director is someone who is able and willing to share knowledge and ideas.

"The best work comes from an art director who allows the team to extend an idea by pushing the boundaries and who is willing to credit the team or individual designers on a job well done," he says. "The other side to a good art director is a comprehensive and up-to-date knowledge and understanding of the print and production process."

Helen Watts' passion for her work extends to her leadership of a design team.

"I love to get my designers excited over a certain concept, and I never close a door to their ideas. However, we explore together whether a solution is appropriate by asking a series of questions related to our target market, the budget, the effectiveness, and client objectives," she says, noting that she only brings her ideas forward as suggestions. "This allows the designer to go through the process of furthering these ideas and disregard the ones that won't work. The designers have more ownership and pride in their work."

Helen also likes to share the print production variations to explore the available outcomes. With many years of experience and of experimentation, she is able to assist younger designers to consider and visualize the possibilities. But this is not possible unless the less experienced designer wants to learn.

"What does not work is when a designer won't take your comments and is not prepared to explore your ideas or when someone doesn't listen and misinterprets the [client] brief. It wastes valuable time," she says.

Personality also plays a big part in the success of any art director. Peter Watts explains: "There are certain types of people who should never be art directors, no matter how good their design skills are. For example, a person with a large ego who won't allow others to explore their ideas, or someone who criticizes the work of other designers in non-constructive ways should not be an art director."

Another fatal fault: Some art directors don't pay attention to detail. They don't fully brief their designers on crucial elements of a project, like budgets or timelines or key messages. They also might pay less attention than they should to the client brief, or blame others if the project goes off the rails.

Another way to "art direct" is to work closely with professional design organizations and their members. Helen was president of the Australian Graphic Design Association for five years, stepping down only recently to devote more time to her business.

"I spent a lot of time presenting to university students around Australia, helping them prepare for a career in our industry," she explains.

FOSSIL, INC.

Directing Art and Hearts

For Tim Hale, art direction is all about steering people on human as well as creative levels. It is not about forcing his own opinions or aesthetic on others, nor is it babysitting. He knows that without proper staff training and selection, art direction can be a losing battle.

He serves as in-house creative director to about fifty designers and twelve art directors at Fossil, the watch company known for years for its innovative and consistently evolving design. Despite an amazing level of output from his department, what strikes you about Hale is that he is calm and confident. The secret for staying balanced is no secret, he says.

Tim Hale's goal is to create an environment that always shows his staff the level at which the creative bar is being held and to have the proper processes in place that help staff easily clear that bar. He does not have time to handhold, or worse, help fix work that has somehow gone off track.

"It's pointless," Hale says, "to over–art direct any staff member: They will never have a chance to learn if you are doing that, because they will never understand the reasoning behind decisions."

Also fundamental to his philosophy of art direction is that it is not done to make people do things his way: Instead, he stresses doing things the Fossil way. What he requests from his staff is justifiable direction from a business plan standpoint.

Art direction, he says, comes down to respect among peers. It goes beyond pure design sensibilities and relies heavily on the relationships his team has in place.

"When you have built a team, it is much easier to art direct. In creative circles, it is often the opposite situation: There is a lot of competition. But in a team culture, you can deal with people on a professional as well as human level. That is the ideal," he notes.

For Fossil's creative department, team building starts with hiring the right people. Hale is fairly restrictive when it comes to bringing new designers on board. He is looking for three things: maturity in problem-solving, good traditional skills, and a willingness to learn.

People with developed problem-solving abilities are able to resist a rote mentality. They never stop thinking creatively. Hale knows that, as designers progress through their careers, and especially if they are working on the same basic product and promotional mix as part of an in-house group like his, they can lose their creative edge. So his office has systems in place to help prevent that erosion.

"About once a month, we get the whole staff together and recognize good work, work that exemplifies where we want to be going. We will also put on a pedestal work from other shops that we admire," Hale says.

As incentives, Hale offers attendance at conferences and design camps for people who show a propensity to contribute. The department has also conducted team-building seminars, including an intensive ropes course, to learn how to respect and respond to each other.

After he has hired the right people, incentivized them, and then made it clear what the company expects in terms of creative output, Hale must have the proper processes in place to allow his team to actually produce deliverables.

Fossil has a three-step process. First comes research, which includes getting all necessary information from the client—in Fossil's case, clients are primarily represented by the different segments of business the company is involved in, from watches to apparel. The Fossil design group has five core teams, which are additionally subset to support more than a dozen brands. Each brand or product category requires research on the specific demographic target, stylistically what will match that demo, price range, the competition's approach, and more.

Then the team moves to ideation. This involves interpreting the collected data and developing creative concepts that take that information into consideration. The target is to develop concepts that address those specifics without losing sight of a particular brand or category's established assets. With comps in hand, concepts can be taken to the client for further evaluation.

Finally, execution—the actual production of the project—can begin. Hale knows that these three steps are not unique to his group. But by clearly outlining it to his staff, he hopes to prevent reactionary design. "We train our designers to be thinking all along the way, not just reacting to information. If we are held accountable to the process, art direction and design is not about 'I don't like that color,' or anything subjective like that," he says.

Reinforcing this discipline in the way they work also has the side benefit that their clients understand that they really are committed to finding and delivering solutions, not in just making things pretty. This has played an important role in establishing credibility and respect with their business peers.

But as creative director, even with all of these systems in place, Hale is sometimes called in to give the final word on a design. Then it's time to step away from his opinions.

"Steven Covey talks about finding a third alternative. I may not like what they did and I may already have an opinion in my head about how it should be done, but I have to talk about another place where we can go with this thing. It can't be all about them or all about me," he says. But if he does have a strong opinion about something, he will voice it. "I will try to point out that direction, but it has to be supported by a good reason why."

Art direction is very much like coaching, Hale says. There are situations where he has to insist on a certain direction, and if an individual designer can't handle that, then it is the art director's job to explain the reasons for that direction. If a designer is unable to grasp those reasons, then long-term, perhaps this is not the best team for him or her.

One of the most important things an art director can do is to teach his or her staff to remove the personal aspect from problem-solving.

"It comes down to not hurting someone, especially a young designer. It is not about them—it is about coming up with a good solution for the client. Clients must depend on designers to do the right thing for them. It's my job to straddle the fence and look at the situation from both the client's and the designer's standpoint," he explains.

Yes, art direction can have its dictatorial aspects: Discipline must be consistent in order to keep creativity from wandering astray.

But any such direction must be kind and measured as well. "If you have a studio full of creative people and you're not utilizing that creativity, what are you paying them for? You are not taking advantage of their collective talents," he adds.

VRONTIKIS DESIGN OFFICE

The Gentle Leader

Much of Petrula Vrontikis' inspiration for art direction comes from her role as a teacher at Art Center College of Design. She balances compassion with administration, offering ideas but not solutions.

Being heavy-handed, she says, doesn't help anyone. It exponentially increases the art director's job, and the designer learns little, and so is increasingly unsure and dependent on even more art direction. It's not easy to be a gentle leader, she says. But through example, enthusiasm, and trust, her studio is able to expend its energies doing good work, not knocking heads.

For Petrula Vrontikis, principal of Vrontikis Design Office, teaching has been a humbling and helpful experience as it relates to her other roles as creative director and principal of her thirteen-year-old firm. It forces her to articulate to a young and likely very sensitive designer what's not working in a design, and then instill an enthusiasm for revising it. The difference between heavy-handed art direction and the interpreter role she plays is like comparing the difference between handing someone a plant or a seed for a garden: Either option produces results, but she prefers that her staff be planting and nurturing the seeds of ideas she gives them. They are not just obediently installing fully grown concepts from her desk.

"Some instructors or art directors will tell a designer, 'If you darken this color and enlarge the image 10 percent, then this will be perfect.' I would tell that same person, 'There is something wrong with the contrast and proportion,' and let him think about that," she says.

Vrontikis believes it is her responsibility to translate the assignment from the client's business-speak to the designer's language. She offers parameters and suggests concepts, but rarely hands them her sketches. She identifies problems, but does not offer to solve them for the designer.

Have Patience

Understanding the best ways to work with young designers or students can be an enormous boon to art and creative directors, she insists. For example, someone who is just out of school may be deeply unsure about his sketches. And, admits Vrontikis, those sketches may not actually look that great. But a great idea may still be living there: The designer may just be having a visualization problem.

"In this case, I will ask them to explain the idea to me. That's usually enough for me to give them further direction," she says.

Sometimes a young designer will simply have a different conceptualization process, one with which Vrontikis is unfamiliar. Some students get their ideas right away, some sketch a lot and some write a lot. So as an art director, there is a certain amount of patience that is required, as all designers work at different speeds.

When designers are stymied, Vrontikis tries to remind them of all of the great things they have done in the past. "'How did it feel when you did that one project?' I ask. That's the feeling they need to create again," she says.

To jump-start that designer's thinking, she may pull out books or get on the Internet to find ideas and connections that inspire him and support his ideas. Her goal is to get designers to step out of themselves as graphic designers and try on the shoes of the client or customer. That's where thinking should be re-centered, she says.

Vrontikis is not heavy-handed with clients either. When she hears of firms who give the client one logo at a presentation and say, "This is your logo," she winces.

"We can show them six to eight marks, all appropriate. Then I ask for them to select two to three for us to develop," she says.

Being an effective creative director means being an enthusiastic teacher, Vrontikis insists. The two are so closely interrelated that she believes that people who did not have good teachers in school have difficulty becoming good art directors. Schools often don't teach people how to teach others.

The Crux of the Matter

A good art director also develops with age and experience. As a touchstone, Vrontikis feels that a designer should be moved into some aspects of art or creative direction by age forty. She knows that working as both a designer and as a manager can be a precarious balancing act for some. A manager's day quickly fills with phone calls and meetings, leaving little time for design. As a result, that person's creativity can become thwarted and misdirected into micro-managing other people's work.

It's all about trust, Vrontikis says, in yourself as a teacher and in your staff as talented people. An art director's job is not to give his or her staff just enough rope to hang themselves. You can't encourage them to follow their own instincts and then tell them the work is no good.

The studio owner, despite her gentle approach, does not feel she is being overly lenient when it comes to art direction. After all, she says, as designers improve, the greater the benefit to her studio. "As they grow in confidence and creativity, it only reflects back better on my office and on me as a manager."

WILLOUGHBY DESIGN GROUP
Respect, Perspective, and Stepping Away

As a measure of success for her studio today, Ann Willoughby points out that there are clients and jobs with which she has no involvement. Through careful management and training, other members of her staff are capable of operating autonomously. This was not an overnight development, however.

The key to success for Willoughby Design is hiring the right people to start with. While it's difficult to gauge exactly how well a person will perform once hired, the firm has a successful track record: Once brought on board, designers appear to be happy. The twenty-five-year-old firm has a number of employees who have been with the company for nearly twenty years. The studio's principal offers what she has learned about keeping her staff—and herself—thriving.

Why art direct with a firm but light hand? Ann Willoughby has seen the deleterious effects of what micro-managing can do.

"I set very high standards. However, when I find myself micro-managing, the results are never very interesting. It is much more effective to understand the nature of the problem and make sure we are asking the right questions so that the objectives, goals, and process are clear to the designer," she says. "Design then becomes an interesting activity where we can analyze, synthesize, explore, develop, and so on, as well as learn together."

Discovery and play help the process, she says. Fear destroys it. Criticizing without understanding context or not providing constructive thinking is harmful. "It happens occasionally when my schedule or deadlines have prevented us from meeting enough during the process," Willoughby adds.

People First

The most important asset a firm has, she says, is its people. In terms of economic considerations, reputation, and the quality and quantity of work a studio creates, people are the key to success.

"If you have really great people, you respect them as individuals. Everyone is unique, and if you provide the basics—interesting work, a great environment, a supportive team—then allow them to flourish. A team can do amazing work," Willoughby says.

Being a good designer is all about growing, she believes. Being a good art or creative director is all about watching people grow. There are plenty of opportunities for growth at Willoughby Design. The firm takes a soup-to-nuts approach to design, handling an entire range of project types and sizes. Designers have the opportunity to run a project from inception through completion, which gives them not only more experience but ownership of their work.

The result is that Willoughby designers develop a number of different skill sets. Designers who are new to the office are learning how to handle different types of projects, while those who have been there awhile are learning how to coach and mentor the newer people. This formula works best when the design firm is hiring people right out of school and/or following an internship with Willoughby. In this way, new hires are trained to the firm's ways of working and old habits don't have to be rooted out.

As soon as people are trained, the firm begins easing them in to projects where they are involved in the entire process. Naturally, working with young designers is a challenge. Ann Willoughby remembers a period when a lot of young people were hired at one time.

"There was so much to teach. It was a real challenge for us not only showing them the ways of business and the processes that we follow, but also teaching them how to cope with life and work every day, an eight-hour day—a real job," she says.

Cautious not to over-art direct the new staff and squelch their enthusiasm and freshness, the senior staff was nevertheless responsible for delivering their usual standard of professional work. "We were constantly having meetings about how to have enough coaching, but not too much," Willoughby says.

Although everyone has his or her own style of coaching, the principal believes there are three ingredients to managing designers that help them be successful. First, a creative director has to help less experienced designers ask the right questions so they can approach a project properly. A client's project brief may not contain enough information, and everything the designer needs to know may not emerge even in face-to-face meetings with the client. "Ask [the designers] the questions that need to be asked of the client," she says. "They need your perspective of the project."

Second, the art or creative director must be certain that the designer has an adequate amount of time in which to work. Smart ideas take time, and more experienced graphics professionals cannot expect less experienced people to be able to work as quickly as they do.

Finally, it's crucial to offer feedback from others in the design group and from the client, both during and after the project.

"We ask them what they would do differently next time, rather than what they did wrong this time. This helps everyone learn, and it doesn't demoralize the staff. That's the worst thing you can do to someone in your office," Willoughby says.

All of this training and learning takes plenty of time: It usually takes twelve to eighteen months from the time people are hired to the point where they can truly carry a project by themselves or at least with a team. And since Willoughby Design likes to hire self-starters, as people grow and change, they need to be challenged and given more responsibility each year.

That's when Willoughby's job as lead teacher and mentor becomes extremely important. She must always be setting the stage for ongoing personal growth.

"I want Willoughby Design Group to be a place where I enjoy coming to work every day and that goes for everyone else," the firm's owner says. "I want to be less a manager and more of a mentor along with the other senior leadership team here."

Part Three:

COOPER-
ATING

Section 6: Together, Wing to Wing and Oar to Oar

When You Know How Your Business Partner Looks in Pajamas

Designers who decide to partner with a spouse, life partner, or good friend are putting a lot on the line. Their personal and professional lives become intertwined in a way that few of us can imagine. As the articles in this section attest, the relationship can proceed swimmingly.

But if either the personal or office relationship sours, there must be a way to salvage what is left. Here, you will learn about a married couple whose professional partnership has dissolved but who remain committed to each other; a couple who is together 24/7 and love it; a pair of best friends who have safeguarded their relationship and business; and a couple whose personal relationship has ended while their business continues to be strong. Each offers a heartfelt lesson.

RICHARDSON OR RICHARDSON
Dissolving an Office

Valerie and Forrest Richardson were partners in marriage as well as creative directors of Richardson or Richardson for twenty years. They learned the design business together and built their future plans for the business—together.

A lifelong study of golf course architecture started to consume Forrest's time and passions, eventually resulting in a new career path. This is the story of how their marriage survived and how their business lives were transformed.

So what happens when—after twenty years of working together and building a successful design firm, Richardson or Richardson, Phoenix—one of a pair of partners follows a new career path?

For Forrest and Valerie Richardson, it meant the start of a two-year struggle to redefine their business and their relationship. They didn't want to create the impression that they didn't want to work together anymore. How would they accommodate two very different businesses—graphic design and golf course design—under the same office roof? Would Forrest's new career be a success, and what would happen to the graphic design side of the business with only one partner steering it?

After much soul-searching, the couple took some advice that they had often given to others: "Change is good."

Today, two years later, accepting change has opened many new doors for the couple. They agree that completely transforming the way that they each work has been the best decision they could have made. Valerie Richardson tells her story first.

Pulling Back

When her husband Forrest decided to set out on a new path, Valerie was left to run an office with employees and a lot of overhead—as well as a vision that was based on having two different people running the company.

"After twenty years of working with a partner, now I could do anything I wanted to do. It was all up to me. At first this was scary. Then it became very exciting," Valerie says.

The decision was made to sell the office building and work without employees, from a newly constructed home office. Today, the designer chooses the clients she works with and the type of work she is willing to do. Now that she is concentrating on creative direction and conceptual work again, rather than the administrative responsibilities of a staff and larger office, she believes her clients are getting a better value: her full attention.

Richardson has a team of outside consultants who handle bookkeeping, accounting, and legal issues, and she will pull together teams of designers and production assistants, if a project warrants. But all of these people work outside of her office, which she has found to be very efficient and enjoyable.

Working from home allows her to be more flexible in caring for her family: The couple's seven-year-old daughter no longer has to be in an after-school program until 6:00 P.M. Now she is home at 3:00 P.M. and can be with her mother while she works. Also, the self-admitted night owl will often head back to her office after her family is asleep. That's when she does her very best creative thinking, she notes.

Starting over as a sole proprietor has given Valerie Richardson a renewed sense of self-confidence. Working with one's life partner, often at a rapid-fire pace day after day, doesn't give a person much time for self-reflection. When Forrest switched tracks, her future originally appeared shaky. Now, she realizes that their professional split was one of the best things that could have happened.

"If Forrest had not changed career paths, I may never have taken time to think about what I truly wanted in a career. It's an opportunity that has helped me to be an even happier, more resolved, at-peace person, and in the end, probably a better designer," she says.

Going Forward

Forrest Richardson's new career interest actually developed when, as a boy, he designed golf holes in his backyard and charged the neighborhood kids to play. His interest progressed as he grew—he even wrote and published an international journal about golf course design.

Eventually, while in high school, Forrest interned with a local golf course architect, Arthur Jack Snyder. Today, Snyder is Forrest's greatest mentor as well as his partner in business.

It was his work in designing and writing the golf journal that initially led Forrest to a twenty-year career in graphic design. Was he sorry to leave the graphics business?

"I have always been very passionate about the game of golf. I don't really feel I've left graphic design, though. My palette has just grown in size," he says. Instead of printing presses, he now uses graders and tractors. The ink, he says, is nature with all of its colors, smells, and sounds. "There is a lot of graphic design in golf course architecture—especially the psychology of design itself and how design has an effect on people."

Just Do It

Forrest Richardson's first clients in graphic design came to him while in college. He and Valerie had so much work then that they never stopped to question what they were doing. They just did it.

When the opportunity came for him to design his first golf course, it was déjà vu from twenty years ago. The work kept coming, and he simply found he didn't have time for two professions.

"The reality is that there were different clients to tend to, different organizations to join, conferences to attend, publications to subscribe to, and libraries to keep. Different tools to use and dreams to dream," he says.

Today, his work takes him all over the world. His clients are municipalities and developers, and the land he works on varies from forests and deserts to volcano flows. He must work through home developments, over landfills, and wherever golf is meant to be played. He has also written a textbook on routing the golf course.

While the professional lives of Forrest and Valerie Richardson have come to a fork in the road, the paths they have taken actually have come to run parallel with each other. They still work out of the same office together—although now that office is in their home—and they share in the administrative responsibilities.

In many ways, they have actually simplified their lives. But their ability to appreciate the opportunity that comes with change has brought them to a clear vision for the next twenty years.

PARHAM SANTANA

Together, Day In and Day Out

Divide and conquer: That's John Parham and Maruchi Santana's approach to running a brand strategy and design firm and living together as husband and wife. It's a mistake, they say, to believe that two designers going into business together will both end up being full-time designers at that firm. Other duties will have to be taken up by each partner. Still other duties will have to be given away.

In personal and work relationships, each partner allows the other to do what he or she does best. They complement each other's skill sets and as a result, their seventeen-year-old firm continues to have muscle.

Working side-by-side with one's life partner sounds like a dream to some. To others, however, it has all of the makings of an unadulterated nightmare. Fortunately, Maruchi Santana and John Parham are firmly in the former group. The couple has known each other for more than twenty years: They met as students at Pratt, married in 1983, and became partners in Parham Santana in 1985. They have three bilingual children at home, and they are active in professional graphic design organizations, their children's sports programs, and their local civic council in Park Slope, Brooklyn. In short, they are very busy folks.

Keeping up the pace is made possible by dividing the workload. For them, a divide-and-conquer philosophy works much better than double-teaming.

"It's a common misperception, especially among designers," says Parham, "that two people who do something well can team up and the work will be twice as good. What works better is if what your partner does complements what you do."

The couple has long used an outside business counselor and a full-time, in-house comptroller who tells them how, what, and when they can spend. They themselves divide their hours between managing the creative end of the business as well as sales and marketing. They do team up on meetings or presentations occasionally, but definitely not every time.

Parham works more closely with the creative team in their group, while Santana works more with sales and marketing, which includes servicing accounts and searching for new business.

"I used to be more involved with creative, but I love sales, and clients respond to me. But in meetings, John is very good at closing the deal. Everyone listens to him," says Santana.

She adds that working as a team, particularly in meetings, has another advantage: the ability to coach each other. "John can get very passionate about a project. Later, I might have to tell him that he was selling too hard."

"We have definitely kicked each other under the table," Parham laughs. "But any good working partnership should be able to withstand that."

Being able to graciously give and take criticism is a major factor in a 24/7 relationship. Each has to be able to accept and address advice, whether it is from a partner, client, or even an employee. A thin ego will take a beating.

"Creatives tend to take things so personally. We have to step back and say, 'Why is that person saying that?' and not take it personally. The client's perception is your reality. So creatives have to approach what clients are saying in an honest way," explains Parham.

They keep criticism constructive by holding periodic reviews. Santana and Parham are subject to these stop-checks the same as any other employee of their company. The firm has a review system where a written self-evaluation is requested. The employee and the senior person he or she reports to then sit down for a discussion. This leads to a final evaluation and recommendations that are approved by the partners and the comptroller.

"Companies need a review process and procedure so everyone can grow. This should include job descriptions and a clear definition of who reports to who," says Parham.

The couple advises anyone who is considering going into business with a friend or life partner to, first of all, treat the new partnership seriously, not like some kind of "let's see how it goes," operation. Get it clear and on paper in the first week, and secure financial and legal advisors right away.

Parham says a tentative approach indicates a flaw in the business plan. "It was all out when we started. If you think what you are starting will fail, then it will fail."

"As two we are better than one," Santana adds. "Our plan was, 'Let's go for it.'"

The couple also advises starting as and staying equal partners in the business. Take what monies you have and combine them. Draw the same salaries, even if in the beginning, they are miniscule. But everyone should get paid something, they say.

Of course, since all of their monies come from the same source, Santana and Parham must be vigilant when it comes to providing for their family. They stay conservative and put money away in the business's accounts to cover business slowdowns.

"We do not take all of the money out of the company. We save for our staff and our family," says Santana.

They also have worked hard to save time so that the business and its demands don't consume them. Work rarely goes home for further attention; when deadlines are looming, occasionally they will double-team it so it's finished faster. Business functions are limited to weeknights, and they often take turns attending. A full-time nanny and plenty of calendars at home help direct their family life. Complete organization is the key.

But probably just as important is the need to imagine what the future might bring. "Say if you have two unrelated women who are working together. What if one of them decides to get married? What if one has a child? The future will be more complicated, so you have to be able to evolve as other things evolve—what you 'used to do' won't apply anymore," says Santana.

In fact, she adds, the best way to keep a business young and a partnership fresh is to not think too much about the past. Learn from it, but always be in step with the people you work with, particularly with your own partner.

NUMBER 17

How to Stay Best Friends

Bonnie Siegler and Emily Oberman met right out of college in 1985 and soon became best friends. Both were hired on at prestigious firms — Siegler at VH1 as design director, and Oberman as senior designer at M&Co — but they worked together on freelance projects in the evening and on weekends.

By 1993, they were ready to go into business together, and so opened Number 17. The duo had their first job even before Siegler was able to join Oberman in their new offices (at the very start, Siegler's own apartment), and they have worked together every day since. Here, they describe how to make the same sort of successful fast start they did and not lose their minds or their friendship.

Emily Oberman and Bonnie Siegler's first day of working as Number 17 was the Monday following the Friday that Oberland left her former position. There was no pause, and certainly no time to rest. They never really stopped in the rush of getting the new company off the ground to consider the pros and cons of what they were doing.

Their accountant at the time warned them against going into business together. "He said it was a terrible idea to go into business with your best friend. He also suggested that one of us be the sole proprietor and the other person would technically work for the other," Oberman recalls. "So we got a new accountant. We had to be 50/50 in this."

In addition to securing a new financial advisor, they also hired a lawyer and incorporated in short order. Most important, however, was a set of written and unwritten rules that would preserve their friendship if the business was ever in danger. Today, with six people in their recently expanded offices—themselves, two designers, an office manager, and a producer—they are able to look back at how exactly they were able to get out of the blocks so quickly.

Written Rules

The on-paper rules are simple. They include wills and retirement plans, and they detail what exactly would happen if one of the partners would die or become unable to work.

"It's hard to have to produce this kind of agreement. You will definitely talk about things you don't want to," says Siegler. "But it is so important to be straight about all of these things."

The first precept they established was that they would always be 50/50 partners in the business. And if the company ever broke up, neither one of them would get to keep the Number 17 name. "Number 17 can only exist if both of us are here," Oberman insists.

Unwritten Rules

Some of the partners' guidelines for thriving and surviving are common sense, but they are nonetheless essential. When working with outside vendors for business assistance, pick people you really trust. After all, you are placing your business's future in their hands. They must be part of your team and want to move just as nimbly as you will.

Another tip: Siegler says that in her experience the partnerships she has seen fail have gone down because one partner feels he or she is doing more work than the other person. Resentments develop, and the ground begins to erode beneath the partners' feet. She cites the example of another company where each of the partners felt he was doing more than the other person.

"One of the men was an incredible dominator, and it was horrible for the other person. They were equal partners on paper, but not in how things were done in the office," she says.

From the beginning, though, Siegler and Oberman headed in the other direction: They think so much of each other that they always feel they should be doing more. Today, that ethic has also been passed on to their employees. It pushes everyone to do better, and it establishes a sense of respect among peers.

Another office rule is that if either partner is unhappy with the way a project has turned out, it does not go out the door. They do have different opinions about design, but the job just can't be released until both of them are happy with the solution.

That means that there are inevitable disagreements. As painful as these may be to the friends, they know that within a day or so, they will have to let go of whatever the problem was and move on: They don't have the time nor the inclination to let things fester.

Being able to disagree with the other person is, in their eyes, a plus. In fact, says Oberman, it is absolutely necessary to find a partner who is as passionate about design and business as you are. That means there will be strong opinions and ideas all of the time. The trick is to keep any disagreements on the professional level: The personal level must be respected.

"Sometimes you might be fighting about a job, but what you really are fighting over are personal things. When that happens, it's time to reevaluate the disagreement," says Siegler.

The partners also have an agreement to not talk about money or make any final pronouncements in meetings with clients. They always tell the client that they will talk about whatever is at hand and then call them back later.

"We definitely kick each other under the table, though," Siegler laughs.

Maintaining Momentum

With nearly a decade of solid work behind them and their friendship intact, Oberman and Siegler continue to look for ways to maintain their forward motion. They always have their eyes out for a business partner who could—although he or she would not hold shares equal to theirs— handle the business end of the office. That would make it easier for them to focus on the design side of the office and on relationships with and among employees.

They have also turned their office into the kind of space that makes it a pleasure to come to work. Oberman calls it both a serious and a silly place.

"We just took over the space next door, so now the office is very open with great shelves that actually form walls. Bonnie and I collect funny little things—miniatures, old board games, any object with the number 17 on it, pretty packaging—so these are all over the office. One shelf contains a message spindle that holds every phone message that we have ever gotten since we went into business," she says.

Their conference room has a table with a backgammon board built right into it. When they are stuck for ideas, the partners will go into the conference room and knock out three games. "It's a good break from whatever straps are blocking our brains," Oberman says. The employees and partners try to eat lunch and play backgammon there together every day.

But despite the newly enlarged space, Oberman and Siegler still sit at the same long work surface, just as they have done since the very beginning. It's difficult to hold a grudge, or shirk responsibility, or even be snippy to someone who you know is sitting less than three feet away.

There have been problems, they both admit. But working hard to sustain their friendship has had a very positive effect on their business. For them, the only way to get a business off the ground quickly is to work with a partner with whom you share ideals, not necessarily an aesthetic.

SAYLES GRAPHIC DESIGN
Keeping the Business Alive

Sheree Clark never planned to work in a design office. She was an administrator at Drake University when she met John Sayles, who very soon would become her life and business partner. They worked compatibly together for fourteen years, gathering industry awards and client accolades by toiling almost around-the-clock.

Then, after being inseparable for so long, the couple broke off their personal relationship. This is the story of how they kept the business they'd worked so hard to create healthy and of how they have adjusted their relationship so that the pair can still work side-by-side.

During the same month that Sheree Clark and John Sayles bought an existing building to house Sayles Graphic Design's offices in Des Moines, Iowa, the couple decided to break off their personal relationship, Clark says. It was one of the toughest things she had ever done, but it proved, she says, that their business could survive. The new studio was an affirmation of this commitment to each other as partners. And therein lies the lesson.

The start of their relationship was a whirlwind event, and the pace never slowed down. Over the period of a few short weeks, they dated, moved in together, and started a business. She brought in a phone from her apartment; he contributed all of his art supplies. They both agreed that, in terms of time—the only thing they had a lot of then—they would do whatever it took to get the work done right.

"We worked seven days a week, for no less than twelve to fourteen hours per day. The first five years, we even worked on Christmas day," Clark recalls. "It was knock-down, drag-out work. Not surprisingly, we had a lot of staff turnover in the beginning because our expectations and demands were so high."

Fast forward ten years: The couple had finally built the business so it could run on its own, and all without backing from investors. They got out of the office a bit more—they both taught design and communications classes and became involved in the local advertising club—but even those activities were all about the work.

Neither begrudged the sacrifices he or she made, but over time, just as their business was beginning to thrive, their personal relationship began to change. Clark attributes this to not having any outside interests at all. But in their workaholic mode, they decided to work even harder. "We had always believed that if you weren't feeling successful, then you should come in even earlier," Clark says.

Eventually, both realized that they personally weren't very happy, and Sayles moved out. The challenge now became how to preserve the equity of their hard-earned business in a way that allowed both partners to still work together.

The New Rules

For fourteen years, Clark and Sayles knew everything about each other. All of a sudden, they knew very little and weren't even sure if it was prudent to ask. At the time, they were renovating an old building for their new office space, and both latched onto that project as a symbol of their commitment as business partners.

"What makes for an amicable split or a successful partnership is not a dollars-and-cents thing: It is all about emotional maturity," Clark explains. The temptation when emotions are high is to get down in the mud and get mean, especially if the other person is acting poorly. "But this is the time to take the high road and treat your partner with integrity. You have to know when to keep your mouth shut and walk away from a fight."

Of course, there have been angry words, the same as there would be in any dissolving relationship. Playing the adult is hard. But the important thing to remember is where those words are coming from. Both people have to be able to step away and tell themselves to try again later, when they are not feeling bitter and/or attacked.

Telling Clients

Since Clark and Sayles did not share a last name, many of their clients didn't even know they were a couple. Those who did were loathe to address the fact they had broken up. But it was clear to everyone that something had changed: Clark lost thirty pounds during this period, and the formerly always-at-work Sayles started going out to a different watering hole every night.

Clark's method was to approach others and let them know that it was alright to talk about it. By addressing the matter, it was decontaminated.

It was important for clients to feel reassured that their projects would still be well-taken care of at Sayles Graphic Design. Never, never let the people who write the checks see any kind of messiness behind the scene, Clark advises. It undermines their confidence in your work.

Telling Employees

The couple's split was announced in a staff meeting, but no one was surprised, says Clark. "We invited employees to talk, and of course, no one did," she recalls. But the event was very important in terms of reassuring employees that the business and their jobs would stay intact.

From then on, if Clark and Sayles had a disagreement of any kind, they would leave the office to hash it out so that their staff would not have to listen.

"Fighting in front of the staff makes them scared for you and for themselves," Clark says. "If there is going to be an altercation, have the sense to not do it in your front lobby."

It's also important to not put employees in a position where they have to take sides. This is something that can happen inadvertently: Just voicing your frustrations out loud can poison the water; the employee may feel that he or she has to agree or disagree, and that only spreads the divisiveness. Remember that everyone in the office is struggling with forming a new relationship: Everything is different.

The Aftermath

The reason Sayles Graphic Design and Clark have survived this life-changing transition almost without a hiccup is that she and Sayles have always maintained a clear division of duties and have faith that the other person will do a good job. They still support each other in their work. In fact, during times like these, the nicest thing you can do is cut your partner some slack and even lighten the load, whenever possible.

Clark also makes it a point to compliment her partner whenever she feels he deserves it. "I might call and leave a message at his home to say that he did awesome in a presentation," she says. These are sincere compliments, but she knows that she is salting a little something away in the emotional bank account for possible future use. "Someday when I am in a bad mood and say something stupid, I hope he will remember that I have also said something nice."

Lessons Learned

One thing that Clark and Sayles know now is that they need time away from the work, with interests outside each other and the business. There is no disrespect in wanting to have other aspects to one's life.

But Clark says her biggest lesson was to accept that what might be right in her life changes over time. "What is right now may not be right forever, and that is fine," she adds. Be flexible and adaptable, and most of all, be creative. An unconventional arrangement may be the answer to your problem.

"For us, we believed it was not necessary to have a written-down contingency plan if things sour. We both still believe there are certain things in life that should be able to be done with a handshake or else all of the joy is legislated out of life.

"But," she adds, "Remember that this is a business. You have to be prepared mentally for whatever comes your way and be able to respond without emotions impairing your judgment."

Section 7: Design or Get Out of the Way

How Not to Knock Heads with People Who Are Nearly as Smart as You Are

Sure, everyone wants a smart partner, someone who is a great thinker, designer, manager, and more. But the reality is that, people being what they are, a truly energetic, organized, talented partner can be, well, aggravating.

Put any group of very intelligent and driven people in a room together, and sparks are bound to fly. When those people are designers, add a layer of creative jealousy and/or admiration. The four firms featured in this section show how to build on each other's strengths, not knock them down. It's a learning experience, both from a professional and a personal standpoint.

BBK

A Laissez-Faire Partnership

Yang Kim, partners with Kevin Budelmann and Michael Barile in BBK, an elegant, stylish design firm based in Grand Rapids, Michigan, believes there necessarily must be some knocking of heads amongst partners for a relationship, particularly in the creative field, to work. It's the spark that makes things move forward. If everyone gets along too perfectly, she says, there's probably something wrong with the machine.

Creatively, she says, they are all different: That's why they came together as a group in the first place. The triad is stronger, not hobbled or distracted, by differences of opinion.

A three-person team has its advantages and disadvantages: In voting, there is always someone to serve as a tie-breaker. But unless the triad reaches consensus with every vote, that old saying comes into play: Everyone is accountable, but no one is responsible.

The BBK design team prefers to reach a consensus so that all three partners—Yang Kim, Kevin Budelmann, and Michael Barile—are accountable and responsible. But consensus takes time: Decisions may be delayed or initiatives may not move forward, and Kim worries about the kind of message that sends to employees. But she also says that, left to her own devices, she could make a lot of wrong decisions: "I'm glad," she says, "that there are other people here who can help me."

Each partner runs his or her own projects, and unless asked, the other two people do not interfere. That's out of professional respect,

Kim says. When asked to collaborate, the team members talk until the best ideas bubble to the surface. They will often do something they refer to as "Team Design."

"We might put the whole office on one project, usually at the beginning of bigger projects, to expedite the creative process," she notes. Each person works on his or her own interpretation, then they all spread everything out on the floor and discuss what is working and what is not.

"Creatively, we are all different. That's what we like about the partnership. It makes us a stronger group that we don't all have the same opinions," Kim says.

Since each person is minding his or her own store, most clashes are over business, not creative issues. For instance, selecting an insurance package that was appropriate for them and all of their employees was tough: It was difficult to get to middle ground, considering all of the different ages and family situations of the people involved.

Peacekeeping Strategies

Under the BBK model of business, conflict is necessarily kept to a minimum. All of the partners have equal equity in the company and are equally compensated.

Of course, there are many other business models in motion today. Kim knows of another three-partner firm where one person owns 50 percent of the company and the other two individuals each own 25 percent.

"That's not so great for the people with no majority decision-making power. It's more of a 'feel good' thing for the two people. But I don't like that situation because even though they can't make decisions, they still have to bear the responsibility of the business," she says.

At BBK, the three partners and one other senior level person are called "project leads." They make and maintain all of the client contacts and are considered to be the company's leaders. Once a year, they get together off-site and go over all the issues facing the company. They talk about what they want for the company in the next year and how they plan to get there.

"Initially, they don't feel very helpful—they can actually be somewhat depressing," Kim says of the sessions. "There are things said that I would not call nice, but we have to talk about these things. At the end of the session, we all know that we are coming from a common place. We see that the core goals are the same. So it is reassuring."

On Agreements

An important tool in preventing disagreements from arising in the first place is to get the key "partner agreement" issues down on paper. They are not easy to talk about, Kim says, but they must be written down so that everyone understands what each person's expectations are.

"For example, take the issue of leaving the company—what is your obligation? We say that for a partner, two weeks is not enough. We ask for a year or more. You also can't compete in the same area for a certain amount of time—this is a small market," she notes. "Our salary ranges are in the written agreement, too."

There are other things that should also be on paper: a policies manual, employee handbook, compensation packages, benefits summary, non-compete agreements, and so on. Kim acknowledges that this might sound stuffy and corporate, but actually, these devices are the things that preserve her office's casual, friendly atmosphere.

On Relationships

When selecting a partner, remember that you are going to see this person every day, says Kim. You will go through good times and bad, so you better like them. That is not to say that you must be best friends. But if you don't like each other, the partnership isn't going to work.

"Michael would tell you that a partnership is like a marriage. I don't subscribe to that," says Kim. "You don't have to love the person, and you don't have to spend all of your time with him. But you do have to like him: You will have to deal with him for forty to sixty hours per week."

The most challenging thing about any business is dealing with different personalities, she notes. A partner or potential partner may have a very different way of dealing with stress or time management than you do, but that doesn't mean that he or she is a poor match for you. In fact, those differences can be an effective counter-balance.

"I am a very practical person; I like to make decisions right away. No lingering. But there is another partner here who likes to talk things over and over again," she says, noting that between the two approaches, smarter decisions are made.

It is important to distinguish between personality differences and value differences, Kim cautions. What if one owner sees the opportunity to partner with an ad agency as bread-and butter-work—consistent, steady work? If the other partner thinks that working with ad agencies is abhorrent, there is a real difference in values, and it could spell trouble for a company.

Sharing Duties

Kim, Budelmann, and Barile all got into the graphic design business to do graphic design, not deal with human resource issues or accounting problems. But, of course, these are areas that they must pay attention to. None of them want to take on any non-design job full-time, so they are currently considering a plan where such duties would rotate on an annual basis.

"Running the business and dealing with things like insurance aren't the most fun aspects of our jobs, and these are the areas where we are most likely to get hung up on some conflict—mainly because none of us are good at them," she laughs.

In the meantime, BBK relies on its office manager, accountant, lawyer, and financial consultant for good advice. Designers are usually not business people, Kim says, and they should not pretend to be. Bad decisions lead to bad blood, and they don't have time for that.

"[Our consultants] will often say things we don't want to hear, but they do know better," she adds.

The subject of getting along with her partners is near and dear to Kim's heart, as she and Budelmann were married just last year. Any partner, she says, should be someone with whom you have mutual respect. That person should have strengths that complement your own. Differences of opinion are good, but make sure you are at least singing from the same book. Be flexible, listen, and learn. And most important, keep your ego out of the way.

ADAMSMORIOKA

Divide and Conquer

When Noreen Morioka and Sean Adams agreed to go into business together in 1994, they did not go into it thinking that it might last one or two or even five years. It was a commitment for life. It would take a nuclear disaster to split them up now, Morioka insists.

That being said, she also laughs as she admits to biting Sean on the ankle after he gave her an Indian burn following a disagreement. Neither the burn, the bite, nor the disagreement left any permanent marks, and that's the beauty of their relationship. They respect each other as friends above all else. They can laugh because they trust each other.

The unique relationship between Sean Adams and Noreen Morioka has changed substantially over the years. When they were both new to the design business, working in April Greiman's office in 1991, Adams was Morioka's boss. So when they left there in 1994 and went into business together, they had to redefine their roles in the relationship.

Their first year together was tough. There were personal issues to work through. They both admit to taking criticism and small defeats very personally then. There were male/female issues to sort out. Adams recalls a common scenario:

"I would make an honest comment about some work she did, and she would take it as, 'I am a bad person, and you don't trust me.' But really, I was just saying what I meant about the work. Or she would make a veiled comment that I was supposed to understand and I would miss it altogether," he says.

And almost as soon as they went into business together, they had to deal with a certain amount of fame. Suddenly, everything they did got plenty of notoriety, and they weren't quite ready to deal with the exposure. They were soon being asked to do lectures, and, not exactly having figured out who they were yet as a firm, would disagree about how to present themselves.

Working at Partnering

Finally, the most difficult issue they had to face was the most fundamental to their relationship: how to be partners. What they discovered was that they weren't going to become perfect partners overnight.

"Good partnerships build over time," Morioka says. "And no one ever said being in a partnership is easy. It's like life—everything is difficult. The minute you change your perspective and accept that everything is difficult, it puts you in a mindset where you want to make things better."

Almost since the beginning, they have adopted the philosophy many married couples do, to never go away from each other angry. Morioka recalls being in New York recently when something went wrong back in their Hollywood, California, office. "There I was, at two in the morning, talking to Sean on the phone so that we both had an understanding of how to work it out. Then there are times we agree to disagree, and that's OK."

In fact, when the partners do disagree, Morioka says she almost always ends up learning something from Adams. That's another vital component of a successful partnership, she notes: that the other person continues to teach and inspire you.

Division of Duties

Today, the partner's duties are split up according to their personal strengths, and conflicts are fewer: Each knows what he or she is supposed to do, and the other person stays out of the way. In the beginning, each person felt that he or she had to do everything in order to be contributing properly to the business. Today, however, Adams is in charge of creative, and Morioka manages all client relations.

"When Noreen says we should do something, I really respect that. Every time that other person makes a decision, you are making a leap of faith that she knows what she is doing," Adams says.

Morioka notes that both partners do still dip into each other's areas occasionally, but when the phone rings, they know who the right person is to pick it up.

It's vitally important to honestly discuss with your partner each other's strengths and weaknesses so that the business can receive the most benefit. "For example, Sean says that I never give him enough information. I may not like to hear that, but at least I know now to try harder," Morioka says.

Being honest about the downside of one's job is healthy, too. For instance, Morioka still loves to do creative, but her job doesn't permit her much time to take part in that anymore. That's the fun stuff, she says. Adams says he can get a bit jealous when Morioka always gets to go out to dinner with clients and receive all the accolades. The clients know her, not him, and that can be hard.

Another division of duties that neither anticipated was that Adams has emerged as "Dad" and Morioka as "Mom" of the office. "People here will come to see me with their boo-boo or insurance problem, but Sean is the authority figure," Morioka says. "That used to really bug me, but now I think, how great is that? It's great to work with someone who has that kind of authority."

Finding the Right Person
Morioka believes an ideal partner should do three things: Be a good friend; be a great business partner; and be completely trustworthy. Red

flags will not commence to wave when that person walks into your life, but when he or she does, you will know in your gut that it is a good match. It's corny, she says, but true.

Good partners have the same goals, Adams adds. "If you have a partner who wants to make a lot of money, and you just want to do good work, you will quickly find yourself moving in opposite directions," he says.

Also, don't move into a partnership too quickly. Find someone who can do what you can't: It should be an arrangement where you simply could not pull this thing off without the other person. Having two designers both trying to produce creative won't work: One designer struggling along is bad enough, he says. Two is a recipe for disaster.

"Left to my own devices, this would be the most incredibly dry and boring firm on the planet," Adams says. "If it was just Noreen, the firm would be a circus. We balance each other out."

Like any relationship, theirs requires time and attention to stay vital. No matter how busy life gets, they suggest spending plenty of unhurried time together in order to understand each other. If either partner starts to feel a disconnect, that person must tell the other that a meeting is necessary.

At the time of this writing, Morioka and Adams had been invited to speak at an event in Orlando, Florida. Morioka rarely participates in these anymore, leaving the public speaking to the gregarious Adams. But they both love Disneyworld, and it would be an opportunity for the business partners to get away and have some fun.

So they'll head out together and reconnect. It causes Morioka to think of yet another positive trait for a business partner: He or she must have good table manners, she laughs. "I know I can take him out, and he won't eat like a heathen.

A sense of humor, a sense of humanity: For AdamsMorioka, it's a simple combination that works.

PRESSLEY JACOBS: A DESIGN PARTNERSHIP

Reshaping Management

Wendy Pressley-Jacobs started her design business in her home in 1985. Two months later, she moved into downtown Chicago, and it wasn't long before she hired Bill Johnson and Amy McCarter as her first two designers. In 2000, fifteen years and thirteen additional staff members later, she offered Johnson and McCarter partial ownership of the company. Since then, with Pressley-Jacobs operating as the majority equity partner, the three have been working together to run the firm.

In 2002, the company moved to new quarters and was renamed Pressley Jacobs: a design partnership. The occasion pointed out the need to sit down and reevaluate the firm's processes and management. Amy McCarter explains how the three partners have fine-tuned their internal structure, their working process, and their relationship to one another.

Bill Johnson and Amy McCarter had headed up major client accounts for Pressley Jacobs Design for many years. But in 2000, they became partners. Now, they share in every aspect of management, including the headaches of meeting overhead—recently a concern during an economic downturn coupled with the costs of moving into a new, renovated space.

McCarter says becoming a manager has been an adjustment. "There just isn't the design time that we once had to devote to projects. We are guiding the creative at a higher level now, and there is not much time left for pushing type around yourself—a part of me has definitely mourned the loss of involvement at that level. However, it is increasingly satisfying to guide the creative team and be ultimately responsible for maintaining the highest standard in both our product and our service.

"Additionally, I have a much greater respect today for the art of running a business. The time commitment is considerable. And sometimes the learning curve seems vast. Once we signed a new lease, my role was to coordinate the design and building of the new space, manage its financing, and coordinate the actual move—in addition to the work—all activities not found in the original job description," she says.

Getting Along with Staff

The other challenge the new partners faced was that where once they were just part of the gang at Pressley Jacobs Design, suddenly they were management at Pressley Jacobs: a design partnership. Their roles had changed.

"There are people here who have been here a long time. The dynamics were familiar and comfortable. It's been an interesting and sometimes difficult transition," says McCarter. "Now that we are two years into it, things are starting to feel natural again. The staff has gotten used to the new structure—and they understand and appreciate how a larger management team can be a catalyst for generating and overseeing more work, which in turn provides for a healthier growing company for the future."

The company's new digs help mark this new chapter in the company's life, and the physical environment reflects its new relationships. The three partners now have offices that are separated from the main work area. This confirms the structure for newer employees, as well as for clients, who are also absorbing the changes here. The designers' offices were designed to foster collaboration between people—while also giving individuals a larger space of their own. The new offices provide for adding on a larger Web development team, additional creative and a small digital photography studio.

Prior to the move, the three partners met off-site to talk about the business, its people, the design process, the structure of the office, and where improvements could be made. The decision was made that the design staff did not have the support they needed to continue to work efficiently. As the company grew, designers were having to deal more and more with non-design issues: creating schedules, coordinating print bids, reviewing proofs and going on press checks, handling reprints, sending back photographers' portfolios, and other time-consuming activities. So two production directors were hired on to handle such tasks. A typesetter was also hired, as well as an in-house Web programmer who could provide instant knowledge and expertise in an increasingly requested media—further boosting their capabilities, and bottom line.

McCarter says this extra support has helped change the way they work. "We have made the step from a small, boutique design firm to a larger firm with stronger capabilities all around. We've grown up. Where we once concentrated on a project at a time—today we recognize that we can have a profound effect on the overall messaging of a company. We strive to collaborate with our clients at a higher level, pursuing a more holistic approach to their messaging by considering all of a company's communication avenues. We see it as a partnership.

"We like to think that we encourage a similar partnership style internally with staff. It's about mutual respect and placing value in the people around you. We are very fortunate. We have a very talented and committed group. Our people are what make us successful. And it's important to let them know this—by listening to their needs and their suggestions. Ultimately, it's about giving them what they need to perform at their highest level."

Getting Along with Partners

Johnson and McCarter have a great respect for Pressley-Jacobs. She has a wonderful business sense, McCarter says, and a very intuitive way of listening to and taking care of clients.

"Her creative direction has always been with a lighter hand—she believes in hiring good talent and letting them perform—offering an environment that truly supports the designers' vision. I believe this has been key to the unusual longevity of our staff." she adds. Since McCarter and Johnson are still new to the partnership and are still learning, they have a natural inclination to let the firm's majority owner take the lead in critical decisions. But McCarter says day-to-day the partners' relationship is more like a marriage of equal partners.

"Going into business with anyone is a risk," the designer says. "You have to trust your partners ethically and morally, and have a clear idea of what they are all about before you step into the relationship. Like any marriage, we do not always all agree," she notes. "But we still value and respect one another's opinion."

Taking a page from Pressley-Jacob's book on art direction, the partners brainstorm together—on creative and on business issues— and let each other run with ideas whenever practical. People that are passionate about their work, McCarter says, are bound to knock heads once in a while: It should be expected and even appreciated.

In an effort to stay on top of the details, they instituted a weekly partner meeting—where they set aside two hours to discuss whatever needs to be addressed—new purchases, new business, promotions, employee issues, finances, and so on. Sometimes it just gives them the opportunity to reconnect during a particularly busy period.

Her advice to someone contemplating a new partnership of his or her own? Sit down and explore all of the "what ifs," she says. Understand the other person's values and how they will react to yours. It's critical to trust the other person's judgment. Once your partnership has taken wing, value your people, respect your clients, and, most of all, keep the humor.

PENTAGRAM

To Each His or Her Own Specialty

Pentagram has nineteen partners in five offices. Getting into the club is very difficult, requiring a unanimous vote from all of the other partners. The company has no new business people or account executives. There are only nineteen highly respected designers, and their respective teams.

The arrangement could be a breeding ground for disagreement—nineteen very intelligent, very talented people all with very different working styles. But the business is structured in such a way that prevents conflict. Every partner is regarded as equal; everyone is compensated equally. Lowell Williams, who runs Pentagram's Austin, Texas, office explains how the organization works.

Equality and generosity: Both are key components of the Pentagram culture. It's what allows a collection of what some would call the world's top designers to operate peaceably together, each benefiting from each other's expertise, time, and reputation.

When a new partner is considered for inclusion by the existing partners, the rule of thumb for each is simple: Would I be comfortable sitting next to this person during dinner? If not, says Lowell Williams, then discussions don't go very far.

If an individual is considered as a likely prospect, he or she is brought in as a non-equity partner for a period of two years, during which time the individual is evaluated on his or her level of cooperation, the quality of work produced, and whether or not he or she is embracing the Pentagram culture. Non-equity partners do not own a part of the company yet, but they have exactly the same rights as any equity partner.

"They have the same rights as someone who has been there for twenty years. That helps instill equality. On day one, that person is a real part of the business," Williams explains.

How to Be Together

There are other structural components that make Pentagram very different from other design firms. For instance, Pentagram has a holding company in Switzerland that actually owns all of the five offices. Each of the nineteen equity partners owns equal shares in each office.

This arrangement is also unique in that the longer-term partners don't increase the value of the shares—although it would be to their financial advantage—so that it would become impossibly costly for younger partners to buy in. This instills generosity.

Yet another unique aspect is that each office shares equally in the pooled profits of all of the offices. Each partner is responsible for a specific profit level, and profitability is tracked by partner. At the end of the year, everything is averaged out and the required profits are shared. Anything earned above a partner's required profit is given back to that person in the form of a bonus.

Each Pentagram partner can choose how many team members (employees) he or she needs—or even build or remodel his or her office space—without interference from other offices. So costs for each partner are necessarily different.

Each office is responsible for the day-to-day business, and a legal and finance committee, composed of one person from each of the five offices, manages the affairs of the holding company.

How to Work Together

The Pentagram partners always make sure that there is plenty of work to go around for everyone: That's where happiness starts, says Williams. If one partner is terribly busy and another is not, it is to no one's advantage. So the harried partner is free to pick up the phone and call in reinforcements from another partner.

"If I have a project that has to do with architecture, I would bring to the table a partner who is experienced in that area. The London office can call us regarding jobs in the States, and vice versa," explains Williams.

The goal is to marry partners to the most suitable project at hand, no matter where their office might be. An example: A project currently under consideration is a large chain of coffee shops, says Williams. The assignment is to rethink the next generation of these shops.

"I may bring in a designer from New York and one from London. I would go to visit with them for their advice, but I would still be the partner in charge of the project. There is most always one partner who is *always* responsible to the client," he explains.

Since the company has no account people, the designers and partners themselves not only complete the design work, they also meet with the client, pursue new business, and so on. It's a real selling point with clients, Williams says.

When Conflict Arises

Even with generosity and equality as overhead banners, there is an occasional dispute. This is not a sole proprietorship, says Williams, despite the level of autonomy, "There are nineteen people here, and you can't expect to win every battle," he adds.

To follow the Pentagram model, efforts must be made to keep the partnerships equal. One individual might be a better designer than another, but the other guy might be better at pulling in the huge projects. Another person might be better at publication design or architecture. Everyone is respected as an equal.

Williams says many partnerships fail because the principals cannot agree on the value of their individual efforts. When you go into a business and guarantee that everything will be equal, there will no questions as to how everything will be shared.

A while back, Williams advised a former employee who was considering going into business with a friend.

"When there are two people, I told her, there is risk of conflict already. You have a 50/50 situation, and somebody has to make the decisions. Someone will end up stronger than the others, he or she will make more money, get more work into shows, or something. It is not always an equal proposition."

A triad of partners is a better model. Also, Williams told his peer to partner with people who don't already do what she does. Go with an illustrator or a motion graphics specialist, or someone else who can complement your skills, not duplicate them. That also helps keep conflict at a minimum.

Create a culture of collaboration, Williams says. Be generous. Promote equality. Know when to back off and when to lead. And maybe most important, remember that you still want to be able to sit next to any of your partners at dinner.

Part Four:

GROWING

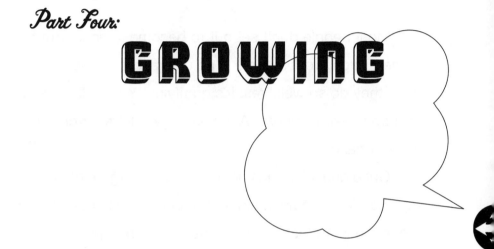

Section 8: Post–Sliced Bread
How to Behave When You're the Latest, Greatest Thing

Most people don't set out to become famous. But for some design groups, fame is an unexpected benefit of what they do so well. Yes, it's gratifying. Yes, it does tend to attract new business. And yes, it can detract from the work at hand.

Once one's firm has achieved some degree of notoriety, the trick is to maintain that attention while not letting it erode the work that captured the attention of peers and the press in the first place. These four firms have achieved varying degrees of attention, and each handles the spotlight in a different way.

CONCRETE

Blind Optimism and Success

Blind optimism is the greatest single weapon against failure in a design firm's first few years, says Diti Katona, principal with her husband John Pylypczak of Concrete (Toronto). When they opened their office in 1988, they had no clients, no connections, and no staff. Today, the company employs fifteen people.

Although Concrete's future didn't look bright in the beginning, it quickly pulled together a successful business plan. In this article, Katona tells how the firm picked up speed and has never stopped moving forward.

Concrete opened for business in August of 1988. By that summer, partners Diti Katona and John Pylypczak had one major client—Reebok Canada—and a handful of smaller projects. It was a frightening time.

"There were times when we were paying our rent at the end of the month rather than at the beginning. We lived in fear of seeing the landlord," Katona recalls.

Soon, clients were giving the fledgling firm trial jobs, mostly conceptual work on smaller projects. Katona says that they knew that clients were biding their time, waiting to see if Concrete would last. Word of mouth kept bringing in small jobs, enough to sustain the partners.

Then, about two years into their venture, the annual reports started to roll in from companies such as Nortel. With the new projects came a raft of awards—from AIGA, *Communication Arts,* the Society of

Publication Designers, New York Art Director's Club, the AR 100, and the British Design and Art Direction Club. In addition, Concrete work began making regular appearances in design publication annuals and awards shows. With that attention came plenty of invitations to address design conferences and judge shows, most recently for Katona, the Clio Awards.

One might assume that this influx of work and attention was brought about by strenuous marketing and promotional efforts. But actually, just the opposite is true.

Show, Don't Tell

Concrete employs fifteen people, none of whom are sales staff. Its principals firmly believe that you get work by proving yourself, not by calling people and trying to sell to them.

"We do not solicit work, and after all of this time, we don't want to. We don't phone around. People have a hard enough time under-standing exactly what it is graphic designers do," Katona says. The best way to instill trust is to show them good work, not to try to describe it or explain that you can do good work, she adds.

She cites the example of Concrete client Keilhauer, a contract seating firm with four factories in Toronto. When her firm first started doing work for the client, Michael Vanderbyl was doing what Katona calls "the serious stuff," such as catalogs and the company's identity. Concrete was handling small conceptual projects, such as a yearly calendar.

About five years into their relationship, Keilhauer created a new chair. "It had no name at the time, but they asked us to do a brochure to announce it. They didn't ask us to do the name, but we called the chair 'Tom' and wrote an entire story around it. They loved the work, and now we do all of their projects, including re-doing the logo, selecting the fabric and color for their chairs, creating a video for the company's showroom, and more," Katona says. "We showed them that we could think of their needs as a whole package, not just individual parts. We showed them that being conceptual meant 'We think.'"

On Being Humble

Katona admits that when she got started in the business, she thought she knew more than anyone else, especially clients. Arrogance is a great survival technique for a young designer—often it's the only thing between him and utter dejection—but it can chase jobs away.

Designers can go further faster just by listening to what their clients are saying, Katona notes. "You don't necessarily have to do everything they say. There is a lot of arrogance in this business: Designers think the client is stupid, and clients think the designer is too creative. If you are pitting yourself against the client, though, you are working against your success."

Self-criticism is another vital component to succeeding. Just getting your work into shows and having other people compliment you won't help creativity develop or keep your work fresh. If you are making your money on creative and not on mark-up, Katona says, then you know that you are truly selling quality work. If that's not happening, then it's time to take a sharp look at one's output.

Running a firm was a real wake-up call for Katona and Pylypczak. She says she learned how to really work. She learned that there would no longer be three people in front of her watching out for her, as was the case when she was someone else's employee. Designers are renowned for overthinking their work, but she learned to make decisions quickly.

The hardest lesson has been the most humbling. "If things don't work out, it's my fault. There's nobody around to coddle me anymore," she says.

Clients and Compensation

Design firms that want to grow should be looking for clients who are confident. Indecisive clients hold up the entire game, impeding forward progress.

"A confident client will see your confidence as strength, not as arrogance," Katona says, who goes on gut instinct when deciding whether or not to work with a particular client. "If I feel uneasy, I don't go with them. Especially when you are young and working on blind optimism, you don't know that there are a lot of creepy people out there who think they should have your ideas for free."

Never, never work on spec, she says, and avoid people who are out shopping. "It's a power trip for these people who give out a few thousand dollars to several firms and say, 'Give me a cover and a spread.' They are just out on a spree, trying to get you to give your ideas away."

Even after Concrete's first summer, when its partners had almost no jobs and no income, they refused spec work. It was worth it, Diti Katona says. Today, they have a reputation as a firm whose work has value.

VSA PARTNERS

Leveraging Growth through Notoriety

When VSA Partners was founded in 1982 by three principals and a handful of employees, it didn't immediately rise to stardom. Like all young agencies, it took some time for VSA to become a darling of the design press for its innovative work. But by 1992, it had earned accolades for its work for such clients as Harley-Davidson, Ingalls Hospital, and the Chicago Board of Trade. Today, the accomplishments of the firm have attracted additional partners, exceptional employees, and clients representing some of the best-known brands in the world.

But fame in itself is not the firm's goal. Instead, VSA uses its visibility and reputation as a means of moving itself forward, both creatively and economically. The reason, says partner Jamie Koval, is that they still have the feeling they haven't really arrived. Fame, like trying to be fashionable, isn't a sustainable business principle, says Koval: It's a by-product of doing great work.

The early 1990s were an especially exciting chapter in the history of VSA Partners. The Chicago-based firm was winning national and international recognition, luring talented staff members, attracting media attention, securing speaking engagements, and building an enviable roster of clients. The success was made all the more impressive by the youth of the firm's principals. Aside from founder Robert Vogele, all the partners were in their early thirties. It would have been easy, recalls Koval, to just say "We've arrived," relax, and coast on newfound attention. But taking it easy has never been VSA's style. Instead, Koval and VSA principals Dana

Arnett and Curt Schreiber looked to the long-term, using acclaim as a tool to inspire the firm to an even higher level of achievement.

"The healthiest way to look at fame in the design industry is to understand that it's relatively insignificant in the bigger picture," says Koval. "While it's gratifying, it's a short-term phenomenon. It's not how we measure our worth to our clients."

Fame from the Outside

There's no doubt that a well-known, well-regarded firm draws far more prospective employees than it could ever hire. Applicants see an opportunity to quickly become a part of a success story. That image is soon met by reality: at VSA: Every person on the team is expected to contribute. "If you're a year out of school and your idea has the most relevance, you're just as valuable a contributor as someone who's been in our office for fifteen years," says Schreiber. "VSA is not for everyone. Some people struggle with the pace and day-to-day creative challenges. Others make the leap with us. It's part of who we are."

What people on the outside don't recognize is that every few years, graphic design produces a new firm du jour—a momentarily "hot" office that breaks the mold and gains the spotlight. That fame, as the saying goes, is sometimes not everything it's cracked up to be. For instance, for several years in the Nineties, VSA designers and partners were in top demand for speaking engagements. Koval says the honor of the invitation and opportunity for the firm to gain exposure made it attractive to speak virtually anywhere, from a small group in Milwaukee to a large national conference. But the gravitational pull of the office and client work has always been stronger than the allure of professional appearances, he says, and VSA refused to sacrifice good work for personal acclaim. Today, the partners spread their attendance amongst themselves at various engagements.

"Visibility and speaking engagements are critical. The beauty of our office is that most of us can be working while there is still someone else on the road, waving the flag for us," he says.

Fame from the Inside

Acclaim attracts high-profile opportunities, which is gratifying in itself. But while VSA welcomes these blue-chip clients, it also pours its energy into projects for companies with lower profiles and emerging brands.

For instance, in the business's infancy, it won a great deal of attention for annual report work, and clients began to assume that all it did was that type of work. "So we worked hard to expand the genetic makeup of the firm by seeking and getting recognition for more pro-gram-based assignments," partner Dana Arnett recalls. "We never stand still. Moving on to the next thing is what keeps us vibrant. Our biggest fear is to become the stereotypical design firm, doing similar, one-dimensional projects year after year. We would much rather challenge ourselves to find ways to impact a company or create an enduring experience."

It's actually just the opposite frame of mind many firms would have after gaining the same recognition: Having reached a pinnacle of fame, rather than hold on for dear life, the partners at VSA know that the challenge of the next height is what drives their staff forward. Sustaining a reputation also requires a commitment to standards and design integrity, a challenge that VSA faced in the early 1990s when the firm gained visibility with breakthrough annual reports for smaller companies. Suddenly, large corporations such as Ameritech, Campbell's Soup, and General Motors were ringing up, asking for the same treatment.

"In the beginning, it was difficult for us to do the same level of design work for a company the size of GM that we did for a small company. But we learned long ago how to produce great work for big companies," Koval recalls, "and to bring the same caliber of energy and thinking to every engagement."

Fame and Where to Get It

Nobody sets out to win awards with their work, Koval says—or at least they shouldn't. Industry awards come through doing groundbreaking work and having a unique point of view: That's it. It's definitely not the magic answer that many designers long for. It's something that takes an enormous investment of time and energy. Even if a firm gains visibility and notoriety, there's always the lingering question: What do you do next year to top yourself?

"Anyone who takes a good, hard look at their client list and works hard will find out they can change their level of visibility in some meaningful way," Arnett says. "In six months to a year, you can totally repackage yourself. The challenge is to fulfill what you're promising inside that package."

The most enduring prize, Koval adds, is a good reputation. Being a flash in the pan may get you visibility, but it lasts just an instant, he observes. "A legacy, on the other hand, is something you build every day. You don't script it or expect it. Being able to thrive and build a sustainable company is what running the race is all about."

JENNIFER STERLING DESIGN
Ignoring Fame Altogether

Jennifer Sterling is a designer who has enjoyed a great deal of media attention in recent years. Her clear, concise work is understood and appreciated as much by clients as it is by peers, and it has not gone without attention. Awards are plentiful, and her current client lists includes Nokia, Yahoo!, a coalition under the direction of Hillary Clinton and Madeline Albright, as well as the launch of her own product line, Hello Jennifer.

But fame is really the least of her concerns: In fact, she doesn't really enjoy it. Entering shows is done to attract clients to her business, pure and simple. It is not done to garner the admiration of peers.

As the old saying goes, fame has its price. For Jennifer Sterling of Jennifer Sterling Design, San Francisco, a recent measure of that price could be that a book on her work (to be published by Ginko Press) is two years late in production. There just hasn't been time to deal with it.

She's nonplussed by the attention her firm's work receives. In fact, Sterling was extremely reticent to even discuss the subject for purposes of this article: It really isn't an issue for her. "I actually just enjoy designing. I also very much enjoy client interaction in the creative area," explains Sterling, whose work was recently the subject of a three-month exhibition at the San Francisco Museum of Modern Art. In addition to winning almost every known design award and being nominated in 2001 for the Chrysler Award and the National Design Award, her designs are in the permanent collections of the Library of Congress, The Smithsonian, the Cooper-Hewitt National Design Museum, Museum Fur Kunst Und Gewerbe Hamburg, the San Francisco Museum of Modern Art, and Bibliothèque Nationale de France.

It's not that she doesn't enjoy being in the limelight, but has learned two valuable things about fame: It eats up a lot of time, and it also invites commentary, good and bad.

"As far as media attention [is concerned, I] think the more someone's work is published, the more available they are to criticism and accolades," she says. Her firm submits work to design shows to gain client attention and possibly procure future work. But when the work wins awards, it seems to announce open season on editorializing by peers. She pays no attention to such comments, mainly because they are generally made out of context to the project.

"I think you can truly only judge the finished project by experiencing the client's goals and the interaction that takes place in the design process. So ultimately, the client's response to the work and my response to the finished product based on the process is what affects my view of the work," she explains. What she sees as her most effective work is often not what wins awards. "I think some of our best work is relatively unnoticed, and some work that I care for less seems to command a great deal of attention."

That's not to say that she doesn't regard the comment of peers as valuable sometimes. But her interest in submitting work in the first place is to serve the client and produce the best design possible, so she stays focused on that.

The Pluses

Of course, fame has its payoffs. Sterling has never had to cold-call clients. They see her work in annuals and such, and they call her.

But there's an inverse reaction to this advantage: The more attention she gains through shows, the more clients she has. The more clients she has, the busier her office is. But the busier her office has become, the less time she has to enter awards shows.

"We completely missed last year," Sterling says. All of the shows she prefers to enter issue their calls for entry between November and June, her busiest time of year.

Dealing with Attention

Sterling finds that being in the limelight eats up a lot of her time: For instance, she finds herself speaking to groups or judging shows at least twice a month. So she is very strict about scheduling. She keeps her office small, just herself, one assistant, a bookkeeper, and usually, a student intern.

"I find this size ideal," she says, noting that it's quite easy for a firm to grow, and much harder to keep it small. "We have been larger, and I felt I was spending too much time managing people."

She also tightly controls the amount of time she spends on business issues. Accounting, scheduling, new business, hiring, purchasing, and travelling are all scheduled for the same day, once a week, every week. She has learned not to mix creative time with business time, and in fact will not even take a phone call or question regarding these matters on other days.

"There's nothing worse than breaking your creative process to wade through the minutia in your insurance policy," she points out.

"I don't think attention should be the goal," Sterling says. "If you work at what you love, success will follow. This should be the goal. Success, however you define it, is just a symptom."

ALEXANDER ISLEY INC.

Broadening One's Base

Alexander Isley is not a flashy designer, prone to grandstanding or out-
rageous self-promotion. What he is is a talented professional whose
influential work at M&Co, Spy Magazine, and with his own firm—where
his clients include Giorgio Armani, Nickelodeon, and the Rock and Roll
Hall of Fame—earned him a solid reputation in the 1980s and 1990s,
plenty of awards, and a healthy amount of press coverage.

He chalks up all the attention to very hard work and very dumb luck,
but when he was first starting up, Isley did do a number of simple things
that helped him first gain client attention, which was quickly followed by
peer and media notice.

Graphic design is unique within the design disciplines, says
Alexander Isley, who heads the design firm Alexander Isley Inc. and is a
partner in the advertising agency The Dave and Alex Show, both with
offices in Redding, Connecticut, and New York City.

He points out that due to the rapid nature of the work, graphic
designers can achieve notoriety and recognition in their twenties. An
industrial designer might not experience the same type of recognition
until his or her thirties or forties. It's not unusual, he says, for an architect to not start achieving wide acclaim until his or her fifties or sixties.

You don't see a lot of graphic designers in their fifties and sixties
still plugging away, Isley says: They seem to gravitate to other fields.
It's a shame, he adds, but its cause is understandable. Much of what a
graphic designer does is so ephemeral that it disappears quickly:

Designers who want to leave a more lasting legacy often choose to do other types of work.

Isley has decided to stay within his chosen field, however, and work on a wide variety of assignments. To serve his clients better, he has divided his work into two separate companies: Alexander Isley Inc. is strictly graphic design, and through The Dave and Alex Show, he handles strategic development, marketing and advertising projects with partner Dave Goldenberg. There is some overlap of employees between companies, but the partners like to keep the businesses separate and focused. In this way, each company becomes well known for its individual specialty, and its renown doesn't become watered down by a host of other offerings.

Capturing Attention

The very best way to get attention, says Isley, is to do work that is interesting and of which you are proud: That's the fundamental thing. But past that, there are ways to stay in the public eye. After opening his own firm in 1988 he first resolved to keep track of his own work: When a studio is busy, as his was almost immediately, it's easy to forget about collecting samples, which are crucial to building a portfolio.

Isley also insists that his clients put his firm's credit on all designs. He sees it as a good way of keeping his name out there. While this is a sticking point with some clients, he says, most go along with this stipulation, and a few even insist on it. He also enters the firm's work in selected competitions and awards, but not as many as when he first started out.

"There are so many awards and annuals out there today. If you win, you get noticed quickly, but it fades away soon. You are only as good as your last project, and that is soon forgotten," he says. But since he knows that some savvy clients scan the awards annuals in search of designers to hire, he continues to enter his firm's work in a few high-profile publications and competitions.

Isley also does a lot of speaking to schools and at gatherings of graphic designers. The audience rarely has potential clients in it, but such events do help to keep the firm's name out there. And usually, one speaking engagement will spawn another.

Another benefit: He found that speaking helped him develop his poise for client presentations. Part of the deal he makes for speaking engagements includes the provision that the sponsoring organization must print a poster of Isley's design and supply him with 300 extra copies, which he mails to prospective and current clients.

Today, Isley and his team aggressively promote themselves through targeted mailings, joining professional design and marketing associations, and through design-related writing. For example, Isley writes a monthly article on design for Reveries.com, a marketing-related Web site. He sees it as a way to reach an audience of potential clients.

Despite all of these initiatives, the firm continues to get the bulk of its work through referrals, which reinforces Isley's belief that the most important thing is to, above all else, focus on doing good work.

In-House Management

Over the years, as his reputation was building and his phone rang more frequently, Isley was careful to build his business very slowly and methodically.

"I had heard too many stories where a business grew very quickly and the overhead became crippling. I hired people slowly, and some of the spaces in which our offices were located were a bit questionable but cheap. I did not want to fall into the trap of having to take on boring work just to pay the bills," he says.

Even today, he keeps his cards close to his chest. With five designers, two project managers, a bookkeeper and himself, he stays tightly involved in all work that goes through his office: Every project must have his approval before it is presented to the client or shipped for production.

A Head of Steam

To keep his name out there, Isley spends plenty of time looking for smart clients. He is less worried about finding high paying jobs than he is about searching out projects that offer plenty of satisfaction.

"You should not lose track of doing work that you are proud of: Everything will snowball from there," he says. "Designers can get sidetracked and look at the wrong things. We spend at least a meeting or two with clients before we decide whether or not we will sign on with them. I would rather not do a job if they only want it banged out."

A smart client, he adds will make the outcome of a job so much better with his or her feedback and ideas. The client makes the job better, then the designer enjoys the acclaim, and everyone shares in the success of the outcome.

It's interesting how designers come in and out of favor with clients, with peers, and with the press, Isley says. From long experience, Isley has learned that fame is cyclical. So he tries not to worry about his level of exposure at any one time. Otherwise, it can be easy, he says, to lose sight of why he went into this business in the first place: to do great design, not to get famous.

Section 9: This Land Is My Land; This Land Is My Land

Opening an Office in Another City or Country

It's a dream that many design firm owners entertain: What would it be like to open another office in another city or even in another country? Would it double one's business, or just double one's chores? How do other firms handle this seemingly so successfully?

In this section, four very different firms tell their stories. In some cases, multiple offices have been a smashing success. In other instances, the experiment's outcome is still unknown. All agree that there must be very sound reasoning why an office might expand in this way, because it spells an enormous amount of work and investment.

TURNER DUCKWORTH

A Trans-Atlantic Friendship

David Turner and Bruce Duckworth, principals of Turner Duckworth (San Francisco and London) are surprised at how their business has prospered. Their fathers, both of whom owned their own businesses and had complete confidence in their sons, are just as surprised at their success. It wasn't that they didn't hope for success: It's just that their two-continent office began in a rather unplanned way.

Even though the friends ended up apart, working on opposite sides of an ocean, they feel that their friendship has grown along with the business. David Turner explains how founding a business on a personal relationship rather than on a business strategy has been the key to happiness.

"We see eye-to-eye," says David Turner of his partner in Turner Duckworth, Bruce Duckworth, who happens to live and work an ocean away. "That's the bedrock of the firm."

The fact that Turner is in San Francisco and Duckworth is in London has actually been a boon to their business and relationship: Too much togetherness isn't always a good thing, Turner says.

"What Bruce and I always talk about is how our friendship has grown stronger, as has the partnership, because we are not on top of each other every day," he adds.

Their trans-Atlantic relationship began almost by accident. Turner followed his girlfriend-now-wife from London to San Francisco, and soon after, the friends decided to open a pair of design offices. Each partner is a principal to his respective firm and a consultant to the other partner's firm. Shared values and going through the same stages of family life simultaneously helped cement the fledgling business relationship.

Benefits Galore

The main benefit of having offices in two cities is that it allows a small creative studio to have a very wide perspective. Like any small firm, they are able to give clients quick, personal attention, are nimble and fast on their feet, and produce very targeted creative. But with its global outlook, Turner Duckworth avoids being a typical parochial, single-city studio, an easy groove to fall into when you are hunkered down and busy with projects.

The partners also get to travel back and forth four times a year, twice in each direction—that feels sufficient, says Turner. Duckworth loves California, and when he is in Turner's office, he is a consultant, not "the boss." So his visits are pure pleasure and a break for him. Turner gets to travel home on an expense-able plane fare and also gets to enjoy some downtime from being in charge. "Psychologically, I am still very much a citizen of England," Turner notes.

The partners have also set up an exchange program in which staff members can go to the other office and work for a month or so. Personal relationships are developed as designers meet designers, and culturally, everyone grows from the exposure to another country and city. The exchanges are always two-way, so either two designers swap apartments or the company rents space for them.

Other advantages: Both offices bring diverse skills to the partnership that can be borrowed when needed. The San Francisco office has more experience in motion graphics and Web design; London has more experience in packaging and has more contacts with illustrators, visualizers, lettering artists, product designers, and so on. Suppliers can be shared, and when business is flat in one country, it is liable to be much better in the other. Overflow is passed on to the other office so that both stay busy all of the time.

Large clients also like Turner Duckworth's international presence. These businesses are able to work with two sets of designers and only one set of managers, which streamlines their projects enormously. And technically, they can be assured that there is someone working on their projects nearly around-the-clock, given the eight-hour time difference between the offices.

The time disparity is about the only disadvantage to the partnership: There are times when one partner simply cannot phone the other. They partially eliminate the problem by having comprehensive studios set up in their homes for before- and after-hour conferences. As broadband technology improves, Turner expects even these difficulties to be minimized. He looks forward to the day when the two offices share video windows so that the staffs can observe even mundane day-to-day operations overseas.

They keep other time-difference problems to a minimum by staying relatively autonomous and not allowing one office or the other to become the main creative or the main accounts management office. The other office is looked at as a bonus resource, never a necessity for operation.

Creative Exchange

Every day, the partners and their staffs communicate frequently, usually by e-mail. But occasionally, the two teams will conduct a "distant crit": The project brief and all visuals and progress for a particular project are e-mailed and faxed for a brutal assessment by their overseas counterparts. Even Duckworth and Turner's work is subject to these reviews.

"The crits have been very helpful in raising the design standard. We do get some really good opinions when people see things fresh like that, and the distance really helps. If a design works in both places, then you know it is a good design," Turner says.

The crits take Turner back to his college days when one received a full and thorough going over by one's peers. If you are only getting comments from people in your immediate office, he says, they tend to be too kind.

Financial Exchange

Duckworth and Turner have set up their partnership so that each office is separate. They are 50/50 partners in each office, but their financial split is unique: Each takes a 75/25 split. At the end of the firm's financial year, Turner takes 75 percent of his office's profit and 25 percent of Duckworth's. The arrangement is reversed for Duckworth.

"We hit upon this formula by accident. In terms of making money, we don't want one partner to be resentful if he earns more than the other and has to give it all away. But we want both partners to be concerned about the profitability of the other office," Turner explains. With this arrangement, there has never been any resentments, he reports. If one partner does well, he does well, and the other person gets a piece of it, too.

Would they ever set up another office, given their success thus far? The partners do talk about opening a third office in New York or Australia. But it won't happen just because they decide, for strictly business reasons, they need an office in either of those regions. They will have to know or meet someone elsewhere with whom they can form a close personal relationship.

"Wherever that person lives is where the new office will be," Turner says.

DESGRIPPES GOBÉ GROUP
Logical Worldwide Expansion

For Marc Gobé of Desgrippes Gobé Group (formerly DGA), a company with six offices in six cities around the world, geography was a very relevant factor in deciding to open a new office. To be in the Americas, Europe, and Asia to support clients was key.

This worldwide presence has taken years to establish. Proper management had to be in place, as well as long-term financial support since the new location would be a drain on the parent company for several years until it found its feet. In this article, Gobé details how his company has grown to employ over two hundred people worldwide and continues to expand.

In the early 1970s, Joel Desgrippes founded a brand design agency in Paris, specializing in corporate identity, packaging, and retail environments. It was a new idea in France and a concept that succeeded immediately, particularly with beauty and fashion clients interested in building brands worldwide.

In 1980, after eight years of professional experience with his own San Francisco–based firm, Marc Gobé joined Desgrippes as a partner to form Desgrippes Gobé. Their specialties were the beauty and luxury goods industries—makeup, fragrance, clothing, and much more. Clients included Esteé Lauder, Godiva, Dior, and Hermés, but very soon the new firm was also asked to consult on extensive design programs for the Winter Olympic Games in Albertville, the French Bank Credit Lyonnais, and the Tour de France.

Their extensive experience in these niche markets and pressing demand from American clients to work with the group led them to the almost foregone conclusion that they should open a second office in New York, another hub of the beauty and fashion world, which they did in 1985. That new location prospered, and in 1990, the partners had the opportunity to open another office in Tokyo.

"A young marketing professional, Cristophe Perez, presented us with a business plan, believing he could create an office for us in Japan. He did, and he also opened a smaller office in Seoul to service Korean clients," Gobé recalls.

From there, the Desgrippes Gobé Group reach continued to extend outward. In 1993, the company bought an existing design office in Brussels (Carre Noir), and in 2001, an office was opened in Hong Kong.

Finding the Right Spot

The success of all of the offices is intimately tied to the qualities of the marketing professionals who founded or who were placed in each of the offices.

Gobé explains: "In Paris, we were already successful. In New York, we had been successful. In Brussels, we bought a firm that had a management with a proven record. In each office, it is the quality of the people, not the location, that makes it a success. We are generally looking for entrepreneurs who want to expand their own base or, given the chance, to create their own organization."

Everyone involved in Desgrippes Gobé Group is expected to stay in very close communication with every other office. They share weekly financial and business reports by conference call and e-mail. In addition, twice yearly conferences bring all of the managers face-to-face to discuss more fundamental issues.

"Reporting is very tight. Everybody knows what everybody else is working on," Gobé explains. When you work with global clients, the important issue is to manage the client needs with the same aptitude as you would local clients.

In addition, as principal, Gobé travels from his New York–based office to outlying locations five to ten times per year. He enjoys the travel, as it constantly exposes him to other cultures and people. Everywhere he travels, he brings back packaging samples as well as photos of billboards, stores, and people on the street, all in an effort to get a feel for the trends that impact different geographies.

Finding the Right Reason

Why would a company go through all of the expense and trouble of setting up an entirely new office? After all, any new office is a financial drain on the parent company, to the extent that it could take the entire operation down if it does not succeed. The new office takes up more time; it has to be visited occasionally; it has to be supervised; more people have to be hired; and so on.

Another particularly ticklish situation is also possible: If a client working with one of your offices becomes unhappy with services rendered, he or she is likely to be unhappy with the entire operation.

It's all about servicing clients well, says Gobé. His firm has a strong specialty in the luxury and beauty industry, so he wants his people to be where his clients are. Even in an age where electronic communications help connect people who are far away, cultural differences need to be understood. Allowing a client to work with a local staff is critical even if the management is in a distant home office.

What is not relevant is geography as a strategic element: Gobé does not see having offices in various cities as a power trip or as something with which to impress peers.

"No matter where you go, you will find yourself faced with an enormous amount of competition. But when you are dealing with a global client, and you can tell them, 'We have an office in Europe,' that may be enough to get you the business. Then it is worth the risk. Or you might have a relationship with a client on the West Coast. If you ask them, 'If we moved to where you are, would you give us more work?' you might find that you get all of the work," Gobé explains.

But the services you offer have to be wanted in the new geography, and the competition that is already there can't be too overwhelming.

Proper financial support is also a significant concern. Outlying offices are a long-term investment: As an example, Gobé says it took his company three years of investment and belief to make his Tokyo office profitable. Be prepared, he says, to fully support the new office for a number of years. If those monies are not available, then the parent company is not ready to expand.

Gobé says that in his twenty-plus-year adventure with Desgrippes Gobé, the thing that has surprised him most is how fantastically people can succeed if they offer the right idea and the necessary structure. He believes that Desgrippes Gobé is "the right idea," but it has to be offered to the right people.

"You may have someone with a very valuable portfolio who is just not insane enough to start his or her own business. So it is interesting to see how a few professionals can grab on to what we offer and succeed beyond their wildest dreams," he says. "The value of what they can produce through an extended organization with a wider client base—I would not have believed it, and I know they would not have either."

In any service organization, no matter where it is in the world, people are key to success. A great professional designer might not make a great manager or business founder, so finding the right entrepreneur is the most important task in reaching success for his organization, he says.

JOHNSON & WOLVERTON
Getting Started Overseas

When partners Alicia Johnson and Hal Wolverton moved their office from New York City to Portland, Oregon, in 1991, their goal was to get into a locale where they could think, rather than just react to the stimuli of city life. Although the move helped Johnson & Wolverton define its voice creatively and established it as a leading U.S. firm, the pair soon discovered that perhaps they could stand a bit more stimuli.

That's when the idea of opening a European office started to sound appealing. In this article, Alicia Johnson shares the reasoning behind their decision and tells how to keep two offices on two different continents united as one entity.

Amsterdam, a beautiful city with a long design history and where art is a part of life, held plenty of appeal for Alicia Johnson and Hal Wolverton, partners and principals in Johnson & Wolverton. The city was also a European business hub, which meant that many companies had offices and business opportunities there. English is widely spoken as a second language, and the Netherlands is very pro-American when it comes to business.

When one of the firm's partners and one of the mainstay designers announced that they wanted to move to Europe—a designer with whom the partners wanted to maintain contact—the time had come to open a new office overseas. (The firm already has a New York sales office.) After living and working in the same apartment space for several months as they looked for more permanent space, in 1999 the designers found a beautiful space one block off the city's main canal—two floors in what Johnson describes as a set of paired, funky old buildings.

So began an exhausting period in the principals' lives. Heath Lowe, the designer who wanted to move to Europe, went to Amsterdam and began to lead the new office, now populated by seven employees. But Wolverton and Johnson found themselves jetting back and forth regularly.

"When we describe this to people, they think it sounds really good, but it's not so easy to pick up and work somewhere else for six weeks—that's about the minimum, humane amount of time to make the trip over [the Atlantic] worth it," says Johnson. Today, the transitioning has grown easier, and as the company's lead businessperson, she is the only one travelling often. Even so, last year she found herself in Amsterdam about nine months; the year before that, she was there a total of five months.

"I never had any idea I could be so tired," Johnson says. "It's like having your first kids be twins. It feels like we are running two separate businesses, not two aspects of the same business." In addition, there is a natural downside to travelling between two offices: Johnson says she sometimes feels like she is not part of either office. "But the wonderful upside is the objectivity I get when I get into a long-term rhythm in either office. I have a sense of possibility for what either office might be doing. It's an opportunity to see the business fresh all of the time."

Other Pluses

She has been amazed at how the Dutch culture has taken hold of her and how it has affected her creativity. Watching the United States and in particular its politics has given her a very different perspective on her work. It's important to leave home to see what it truly is, she has found.

In 2001 and 2002, when the U.S. economy has been slow, the European economy has been more stable. Two years before, however, the United States held more promise in terms of business. Working on two continents gives Johnson & Wolverton a nice balance of opportunities.

Having offices in two cities gives clients and the firm's designers two "home bases" from which to work. For instance, at the time of this writing, a fashion client from Europe had come to shoot photos in the Portland area for its 2002 campaign. "We had a really good snowfall here, and there was no snow in Europe at the time," explains Johnson.

"The other thing that can't be undervalued," Johnson says, "is that there is a real perceived value in clients' eyes that we have a European office." She says the size of their clients has stayed about the same, but the scope of the projects they are given has increased. "There is a different depth now. Instead of being one of three firms working on a brand, we are now more often the lead agency."

Hitches and Solutions

Of course, running two offices is bound to have its difficulties. One of the biggest snags is a lack of synergy. In fact, in no time at all, Johnson says, some degree of competition can develop.

"The logical, intuitive way to run a business is to empower people to run their own show. But autonomy without central accountability leads to islands of information," Johnson says. Those islands could contain creative, financial, managerial, and even personal information. With no system in place to share knowledge, the offices' efficiencies could easily have been lost.

"A good example are Dutch reporting and U.S. reporting of finances. The governing and financial bodies don't interact. We needed to create an umbrella system that allowed us to give the same accounting requirements to both governments," she says. "In many ways, this tiny, little company is behaving like a multi-national."

Plenty of effort goes into maintaining synergy between the offices. The Amsterdam office opens later and the Portland office starts earlier, so that there will be more crossover time between business hours. Umbrella announcements are made regarding vacations and holidays so that every member of the staff knows who will be in the office and when.

Of course, e-mail and on-line conferencing helps a great deal; DSL is a must. Digital photos of sketches and other work are fired back and forth frequently. But Johnson & Wolverton has found a simple but effective way of using electronic communications together with some old-fashioned pushpin boards to stay in touch visually. Johnson calls it "mirroring."

"Every wall in the offices is built of some sort of material that you can put pushpins into. And on any given project, there is a wall where the status of that project is apparent—where all of the research and the evolution of the job is posted," she explains. "All of the characteristics of the project are there."

As the project develops, e-mails and even digital photos of the entire wall are sent to the other office, to be posted on a "mirror wall" there. In this way, both offices are always up-to-date on the status of any project.

Structure and Lots of It

As counterintuitive as it may seem, Johnson says, when opening an additional office, plenty of structure is a must. Otherwise, separate offices will begin to act separately.

"There is something that happens particularly in creative, because it is instinctively competitive. In order to have competition, you need to have an enemy. It is natural to develop an 'us' and 'them' mentality, but it is the most destructive thing that can happen," says Johnson. "Things can get really turfy."

A small instance can start to cause rifts, she notes: One office may not want to share information with the other because its employees feel like they are being babysat. Or one office may have worked out a good process and flow for work, but the other office wants to invent its own way.

"It's a big brother, little brother kind of thing. There will probably always be periods of that in any office. Just watch for it, and you can lead through it," Johnson says.

As time goes on, Wolverton and Johnson's jobs as managers grows progressively easier. And as Johnson tells all of her clients, "You do have to give things time." Time, she says, is her ballast as she continues to make decisions from both sides of the Atlantic.

SELBERT PERKINS DESIGN

An Office on Both Coasts

As the old saying goes, be careful what you wish for: You might just get it. In 1990, Clifford Selbert and Robin Perkins, partners in marriage as well as in the design firm, Selbert Perkins Design, began to consider opening a second office on the West Coast. Their Boston-based firm was doing well, and what better way to find more clients than to go where they are?

A second office has increased business, and it has also exponentially increased responsibility for the partners. Now ten years into the arrangement, they are taking a hard look at their decision and its ramifications.

Having just returned from a three-day, whirlwind business trip to China, Robin Perkins and Clifford Selbert are jet-lagged but happy to be home—that is, happy to be in their Santa Monica, California, home. With just a few more hours in the air, they could have returned to their second home in Boston, Massachusetts.

The partners are not jet-setters with homes around the globe: They are just a couple of very hard-working design firm principals with offices in two cities. For the past ten years, in addition to travel they undertake for clients, they travel together every two weeks from one home to the other and back again.

It has been a tough period in their lives, but one they've learned a great deal from. And the greatest lesson of all has been that maybe they didn't actually need a second office in the first place.

Two Coasts

The couple originally wanted to come to the Los Angeles area for two reasons: They liked the creative energies there, and they loved the weather.

"The weather is inspiring in itself," says Perkins. Several clients had also taken up residence there, she adds.

Setting up the second office was challenging, and choosing a specific location within Los Angeles was daunting for the East Coast residents. They knew they wanted to be near the ocean and in a smaller city than L.A. proper, so they decided on Santa Monica. California's inherent energy, they knew would make the two offices slightly different, but the core mission for each would be the same.

The advantages are many: The partners get to experience the best of both coasts and have a wide client base. But splitting time between two cities can be taxing. They depend on all of their staff members to report directly to them so that they can stay up to speed wherever they are.

Today, the West Coast office handles all clients between Texas and China. The East Coast office deals with the East Coast and Europe. Over time, Perkins has come to run the Santa Monica office, while Selbert runs the Boston studio. Occasionally, employees visit their partner office, and some even decide to transfer permanently.

Each office is kept separate in terms of business operations, with its own projects and billing. However, all PR and promotion for the group is done jointly: The company is promoted as a single entity.

To keep the staffs united under the same flag, the partners make sure both offices are sharing their work electronically, and that printed pieces are distributed to everyone once they are completed. The company's work also tends to get published frequently, which also draws the groups together.

"We maintain a very team-oriented approach," Perkins says. "When there are big presentations going on in either office, everyone is aware of it and is very excited."

Each Monday morning, each staff holds a meeting to set the tone for the week, check on everyone's workload, go over the production schedules, and more. That's everyone's compass point for the week, explains Selbert. In addition, financial reports, billing projections, and marketing reports are generated each week expressly for the partners' edification.

A less formal but important team-building tradition is, on several Fridays each month, to stop work early for a staff happy hour. "We relax and unwind together, which brings a sense of togetherness," says Perkins. Sometimes they go to a local bar or restaurant, or they will order staff lunches for new team members, on deadline days, and for other high-energy events.

Reconsiderations

Perkins cautions other designers who are considering opening a new office to be aware that you can't turn your back on anything. In addition, even though you might try to be in two places at one time, it can't be done.

While you are not in the office, Selbert recommends finding a manager or another partner who cares about the business as much as you do. "It has to be someone who won't feel like a third wheel and who can handle the stress," he notes.

But before the first step is made toward an additional office, examine the true reasons you want to do it.

"Are there other ways you could accomplish the same thing such as by air travel and by electronic communications like conference calling?" Perkins inquires. "You don't want to just be adding to your overhead."

A poor reason to open a new office is to impress clients. The partners have found that although clients like to talk about the advantages of working with a design firm with multiple offices, few take advantage of the perks. Yes, it lends a touch of "nationwide status," explains Selbert, but it comes at a great cost of time and materials.

"You really have to have the drive to make two offices work; it is a huge challenge," he points out. The investment is so substantial that Selbert sometimes—in jest—tells peers to forego the new office and invest in a corporate jet instead.

Both offices run smoothly now and each receives awards and new clients on a regular basis, but Selbert and Perkins sometimes wonder if they need two offices anymore. Technology has ironed out the communication wrinkles in the past seven years, and it's so easy anymore to just jump on a plane and fly anywhere a client is.

Maintaining two homes is expensive, and the two-week turn-arounds are exhausting. So for now, they are maintaining the size of the company at thirty people—about fifteen people in each office at any one time.

"We are trying to make things as tight as they can be," Selbert says. "We have been big in the past, and you do have more clients, but it is a heck of a lot of work. We're working to simplify our lives right now."

The partners agree that the experience has been worth it, despite all of the disadvantages. But would they do things a bit differently next time? On this they concur: Yes.

Section 10: Quick-Start Start-Up

How to Get Out of the Blocks Quickly

It's not good enough just to found a new business these days: Now, new graphic design firm owners must make a fast and noticeable start. Otherwise, they get lost in an industry where everyone else is already moving very fast and is doing everything within their power to be noticed.

This section highlights four firms of varying sizes, but all of which are in their salad days. Each launched in a different manner, and each has pulled business and acumen together in such a way that it will likely survive. Learn what the principals of these new enterprises worried about prelaunch, how they handled those concerns, and what they have learned in the interim.

WINK

Becoming Vested in Yourself

For Richard Boynton and Scott Thares, founders of the fledgling design firm WINK, the moment of realization that they had "arrived" as a company that was respected by clients was in a presentation where they realized that everyone in the room was looking at them. The client wasn't looking to someone else in deference. They were the ones in charge.

It's a strange feeling, they say, when everything you wanted and hoped for begins to come true. Of course, their journey thus far has not been without struggle, and they know that there is plenty of hard work ahead. Here, they share the details of their successful lift-off and their flight plan thus far.

To succeed in a new business say Richard Boynton and Scott Thares of WINK, Minneapolis, is not to be goal-oriented but to be success-oriented. Anyone can have goals, they say: There is only a handful of people who actually achieve them.

In 2000, the duo decided that they could be counted among the latter group. They left their respective jobs, and moved into a 10' x 10' space with no clients and a shared vision.

"The only goal we ever had was to do good work," says Bonyton. The work was what excited them from the beginning: That was the design side of their challenge. Being able to pay themselves a decent wage that would allow them to keep their philosophy alive would be the business side. The second component has proved to be the most challenging.

"There is a golden hour when you are inspired to do your best design. When those occasions arise, you just have to drop everything and focus on the work" says Boynton. "You will just have to come in after hours and do all of the administrative stuff."

Organization and focus, Thares says, is what has kept them going. There is a time to design and a time to run the business. If you aren't keeping things segmented, both components eat away at your day to the point that nothing is getting done.

Why Start a Business?

The wrong reason to start a business, both partners agree, is because you are fed up with your current situation. You cannot be reactionary when you start a company: Instead, you need to have a strategic plan in place, including how to pay yourself, feed yourself, keep the business running, and stay true to yourself.

"When people head off on their own because they are angry, their hand is forced and suddenly, they're responsible for figuring things out on their own. This calm before the storm is essential to utilize because it's your only opportunity to establish a philosophy. Without direction, your company can drift out of control all too easily. Before you know it, you've got issues equivalent to those you sought to escape from in the first place," Thares says.

Besides, the duo say, when you meet with a client for the first time, he or she is liable to ask you why you started your own company. Saying that you were frustrated with your previous employer will not be an adequate reply.

"You need to show that you are centered around the work, not in yourself," Thares says. "Even if you talk a good game, but the real reason actually is that there were bad feelings, it will show through. Clients need something more substantiate."

That being said, even if someone goes into a new venture with the right attitude, she should not get discouraged if she finds herself temporarily overwhelmed with a very bad taste in her mouth. Keep things in perspective, Thares and Boynton say.

"You may feel like you are pulling your hair out, but keep in mind that at least now you are pulling it out for your own benefit and not for someone else's," Boynton points out.

Getting Started

A lot of what the partners did right was in motion long before they opened the doors of their office. They built good relationships with people, including with their former clients. Thares, in particular, brought plenty of contacts to the table, mostly from larger agencies.

The next step sounds obvious, but it's one that many new businesses, in the rush of trying to get established, neglect to do: Let people know that you are open for business.

Get the word out, Thares says. Let vendors, friends, and close contacts know you exist. "Once you lodge your name in clients' brains, they will remember you and hopefully give you a shot eventually."

"Eventually" turns out to be a mantra at many new businesses: It's the measure of time they must wait for the phone to start ringing. For WINK, the first few months were lean. They spent the time casually informing key contacts that they could be reached at a new number. There is a fine line between letting someone know that you're around and appearing desperate, they caution. Every promotional effort is put out there to show clients that you are capable of doing the job.

One of WINK's first successes was with a very large client, Fallon—a job that was landed as a result of one of Thares' former relationships. The monies from that job allowed WINK to take its next major step: The partners were able to start a health plan, hire a lawyer, and secure an accountant—all steps that gave them a more stable footing as a business.

A lavish office has not been a priority for the team, although they know of many other start-ups who believe that this is a top priority. The problem with this plan, Thares says, is that the new office has instant overhead. Immediately, the founders are working for creditors, not for themselves, subverting one of any entrepreneur's goals: to work for one's self.

Boynton feels that a fancy office impresses no one. "Some people feel that it legitimizes them, but I don't think any of our clients care what our office looks like. Most never come here and some don't even know what we look like," he says.

When a small company is overextended, it tends to take on work just to pay the bills, and for designers, that is often not work you love. When you are not doing work you love, the entire machine starts to break down.

To keep costs down, the pair doesn't even have what they call a "kick-ass" stationery system, although they want to have one someday. Life has just been too busy to give the matter proper thought. Still, they feel that their reputation is legitimizing them, not a pile of papers.

The Business Plan

What WINK's partners have on paper is their incorporation agreement and a list of principles for running their business: WINK is about personality, from the work itself to the experience of working with the partners. They want to be thought of as nice guys in a serious business. The work and their environment should be fun—otherwise, what's the point, they say?

Other principals? Let the work speak for itself; don't overpromise; and what you see is what you get. Be understated. Do the job correctly and people will notice.

What they do not have on paper is a formal business plan. They just didn't feel comfortable drafting a document that they would have last them for ten years.

"It's like making a plan for going through a cave you have never seen before: You have to learn as you go," says Boynton, adding that they never put up the pretense with each other or with clients that they have everything figured out. When they run across something they don't know or haven't planned for, they dig in and do the research.

As time progresses, they are getting more and more things on paper. Get your systems in place as soon as possible, the partners say. It doesn't have to be fancy, "just something to represent you when you are out of the room," Boynton says.

Growing Up

WINK continues to grow and learn. For instance, the partners have learned that telling their plans to another person really holds their feet to the fire. The more they talk to each other and clients about where they want the business to go, the more those things come true.

For instance, WINK has not done any special promotions specifically to bring in more packaging work, an area the partners would like to get into. But they have discussed this wish with clients and influential contacts, and the work has come. These informal discussions plant the seeds of growth in client's minds, they say.

As the company grows, Boynton and Thares remind themselves of the reasons they decided to start their own office: the desire to have a stake in a company, to have more responsibility, and to get a bit more credit for their hard work. If they get to the point where they are hiring on their own designers, these aspects will be offered.

Designers are inherently restless in that they need constant validation, says Boynton. This is their art: It's very personal. Being vested in a company is what it's all about. It's what makes the wheels turn.

ARCHRIVAL

How to Cause a Stir

The first news this writer had of Archrival, a Lincoln, Nebraska-based strategic design firm, was when a friend mentioned that there was a bunch of young guys in the middle of nowhere raising hackles left and right. "They're winning jobs away from larger agencies, hiring the top talent in the area, driving cars they probably can't afford—I'll tell you, they are really brash," he said.

As it turns out, only the first two parts of that statement are true. For all their success, Charles Hull and Clint! Runge (yep, with an exclamation point) are what elderly ladies are wont to call "nice young men"—polite, well-spoken, and with plenty of drive. But their five-year-old firm is causing a stir.

Clint! Runge and Charles Hull met at the University of Nebraska as architecture students. What bound them together was the fact that neither had the slightest inclination of becoming an architect. Instead, they were far more concerned with learning to design and communicate in 2-D and 3-D space.

In their third year together at the school, instead of taking on an internship, as the program recommended, they decided to start their own business, creating presentations for local architects. Using everything from traditional boards to animation graphics, they learned a lot—and they captured the attention of three or four actual clients. So through the summer of their junior year, they shared an apartment, worked off the kitchen table, and decided that this was what they wanted to do.

A real turning point for the partners occurred when the university's Center for Entrepreneurship caught wind of these two students who were operating a bona fide design business in addition to their studies. The center asked if they would like to be teamed with an MBA student, who would write an actual business plan for them. With no business skills or background, they jumped at the chance.

The plan was ultimately presented at several business plan competitions, held at the university level, and it won third place at two of them—a respectable finish, no doubt, but Hull and Runge were much more pleased with what turned out to be the real prize: The awards attracted investors.

"These are people who have made their fortunes who just like to help young people get started," Hull explains. "We needed about $75,000 and got it from several sources." They opened an office in a warehouse district in Lincoln. Then, for the next two years, they worked for ninety to one hundred hours a week, all by themselves. They loved their work so much that they were really only billing for about twenty-five of those hours.

But since a lot of the work they were doing was pro bono, they had more creative freedom in what they created. This edgier work began to win awards. The awards began to attract clients. As their client list grew, the partners decided to sink the firm's entire marketing budget into entering design competitions.

It was a successful ploy. The two had always been very confident in their design abilities: They just needed to get noticed. One winning entry in a design publication competition turned out to be a second turning point for the company.

"Lowe's Home Improvement Warehouse requested a bid on a children's Web site. They had seen our work in HOW magazine, and after three rounds, we won the account. It was a half-million dollar account, which was the equivalent of venture capital for us," Hull recalls.

Now, they could really grow their company. Today, Archrival has seventeen employees—all from Nebraska, the partners are proud to point out—and it is getting ready to move into a brand-new space. The oldest employee is thirty-one years old; the youngest is twenty-one. The duo feels that it is crucial to surround themselves with people who are more talented than they are.

"The passion we have for our work comes out when we talk to people, and that enables us to get the top talent," Hull says. "We think one of the coolest things about our company is that everyone is from here. We see so much talent leave the Midwest and go to the coasts. We like to think we have created a real option for talented people who want to stay right here."

Brash Advice

If "Archrival" sounds confrontational and aggressive, it's meant to be. The company is built around five characteristics: rogue, vanguard, disciplined, intelligent, and fresh. Their goals are not regional, but international. They want to do work that affects millions of people.

The "arch" portion of the name is a nod to the partners' background in architecture, but the entire name was a reply to peers and locals who said they would never survive as a business. The partners wanted a name that sounded like that of a band, not an office—something that their employees could really get behind. "'Archrival' had the feeling that it was us against the rest of the world," Hull says.

Are they brash? Hull feels that it is a reputation that perhaps gets exaggerated in the Midwest, where people are expected to pay their dues, not succeed on their own. But the designers definitely want to get reactions with their work. If half the people love it (the client's target audience) and the other half hates it, then they have succeeded, says Hull.

For persons who want to dive into the business like he and Runge have, the number one piece of advice they can offer is, "Lose the ego."

Surround yourself with people who are better than you are and who will support your knowledge base. If your skills in print design are strongest, get someone who is very talented in interactive design, for instance.

"Hire them and then listen to them," Hull says. "Give them ownership of their work, and place incredibly high expectations on them. A good designer who is passionate about design will flourish in this kind of environment."

The second thing to remember is that if you don't have a true passion and love for design, don't even think about running your own firm. The partners still work incredibly long hours. Hull loves the business still, but there were times that even he would have liked to hang it up. Still, that passion eventually has its pay-offs: The team knows that its largest client today was a result of a little pro bono job they did long ago just because they loved the work. Not all work should be done for money, they insist.

No matter what size the project is, they always give it 100 percent, because they know their reputation is on the line: It's a small world, they've learned, and you never know who might see what.

A designer also has to be very competitive to succeed. "We are always looking to see how we can get to the next level. Each project we do should leverage us to a bigger project," Hull says. "We are constantly gauging our work against the best creatives in the world to see how we measure up and to see what we need to do to work at that level."

Archrival has entered The One Show and the Art Director's Club competition, among others, for several years. The first year, the firm got nothing. The second year, it was a finalist, and in 2002, it won a One Show Gold and an Art Director's Club Silver award.

"It's our opinion that if you want to succeed in design, you have to compete, if only to raise your awareness of what great design is," Hull insists.

The next evolution for Archrival is in the works at this writing. It will play off of the Midwestern and rural roots the partners are so proud of, and it will be reflected in its entire branding system, from its business cards to its brand-new offices. There are so many advantages to living in the Midwest, they believe. Why can't great design live here, too?

"We would like to know why the Midwest couldn't become known for design like Kansas City is known for jazz. Our goal is to change that, over time. Or we want to be a part of the driving force for the change in that perception," Hull says.

NO.PARKING

Fueled by Naïveté and Hope

If Sabine Lercher and Caterina Romio, founders of no.parking, a five-year-old Italian design firm based in Vicenza, could back up and handle one aspect of their start-up differently, they would have waited for financing reserved for women from their province. But who can wait for bureaucracy, they say?

The pair is very happy with their direction and progress, despite the fact that they did not have the business experience they now admit they should have had. They got out of the blocks with plenty of enthusiasm and joy, and really, they haven't looked back.

Sabine Lercher and Caterina Romio, founders of no.parking, say that their first few months of business were a bit like playing a game on a Playstation: They were enthusiastic and had plenty of energy. It was a time to enjoy their naïveté when it came to running a business: Ignorance really can be bliss, especially when you're having a lot of fun.

The partners launched their company on a hot, July afternoon in 1997. They had agreed it was time to give their lives "a new professional and existential turn."

"It was almost a bet, a game," recalls Lercher, "to put together our energy, creativity, and intellect, and throw ourselves into a new adventure."

Unlike the other firms featured in this chapter, they did not have a defined plan. But they were both gathered around the same idea: to not become the umpteenth clone of a Milanese agency, where the only focus is money and advertisement. Graphics were at the core of their thoughts: "We did not know precisely what we wanted to do or how to do it, but it definitely had to be something new," Lercher says.

This seat-of-the-pants approach was exciting, not frightening to the two women. Both are graduates of ISIA of Urbino's graphic design and visual communications program, and both had spent several years in the working world. Lercher brought experience tied to the publishing world; Romio had Web design experience, plus had worked for a Viennese multimedia design agency. The final element? "A good dose of recklessness, typical of twenty-year-olds," says Lercher, now thirty-four years old.

It was an exciting time—finding the right name, looking for the perfect office (ideally in the historical center of Vicenza).

These two decisions turned out to be the two best decisions they made, and they have fueled the company ever since.

"No.parking was chosen simply because we are in the heart of the town where you can't park. If that's not enough, no.parking [works] because our energy and creativity can't be stopped," Romio says.

Their office space also inspires them: A majestic, late nineteenth-century, Liberty-style stairway greets visitors at the entrance to the doorway of a seventeenth-century palace. The contrast between the stairway and its surroundings is a nice analogy to the technology the firm brings to a deep sense of Italian culture. It's a particular equilibrium of old and new: If people visit and like the balance, Lercher and Romio know that they will probably be good clients.

Making It Work

The business has been growing for several years, and the partners have learned a lot. Remain faithful to aesthetic goals, they say. Also, impose your style on clients and not vice versa. They only select clients who will allow them to work in this way. They remain geared toward quality and not quantity work.

Their approach works: The partners' greatest pleasure is that they have never had to seek out clients. The work has always comes to them.

The partners felt that they had a great cultural wealth between them, and they would be able to tie that to graphic design. But they soon found that they truly lacked in business management and were totally devoid of even the basics in marketing.

"Our relationships with clients were very spontaneous and actually quite naïve," Romio recalls. "Although this was definitely our weak point, it became an element of distinction. Because we manage to establish extremely relaxed relations with clients, we become a team for which the successful outcome of the work was the common goal. We achieve definite results, not lots of words and planning."

Clients seem to be charmed by their spontaneity and sincerity, combined with the partners' skills and competencies. "They appreciate our devotion to our work and our total involvement in whatever we do," Lercher says. "Our secret is to treat every client as if he or she is the only and most important one."

They have never drawn up a business plan, have no health plan, and don't put a lot of importance in self-promotions. But somehow, life and business is good. Lercher and Romio continue to target clients who leave room for creativity and with whom there is cooperation based on trust and respect.

What kind of work do they get? Clients who do leave room for creativity and who trust and respect their work. Not bad for a couple of "kids," they say.

DOTZERO DESIGN
When Is the Right Time to Start?

Like many new business owners, Karen and Jon Wippich of Dotzero, Portland, Oregon, have been surprised by many things: the amount of paperwork that must be handled, how different running a business is than working for someone else, and how fast time suddenly seems to go.

The couple have made an impressive showing, though, in the three years Dotzero has been in existence. The firm's client list is growing, its work has regularly appeared in a number of annuals and books, and—a sure sign that you're becoming "a name"—it has started to receive e-mails from all over from other designers who want to work there. The secret to a smart start in business, they say, is good planning.

"We talked about starting our own business for a long time before we ever set a date and started saving money," explains Jon Wippich. "Then after we set a date, that time would come, and we just didn't seem ready yet. So we would talk some more and set a new date."

Jon had been operating Dotzero as a freelancer for a while, but he wanted his wife Karen to come on board as well. Their hand was forced in 1999 when the company she was working for went out of business. The couple had planned to start working together in July, but they found themselves in motion in May.

"The thought of not having any money makes it easy to just keep on working for someone else," Karen says. "It is scary, and yes, we were afraid. But once you are there, you can do it. You have to. It brings out strengths in you that you didn't know were there."

It was difficult to break away from salaried jobs, but after speaking to a number of people who had already made the break, they felt more at ease with the decision and moved ahead.

"We finally decided that if this did not work out, we could always go back to work for someone else," she adds. "But we sure don't want to now."

Getting Started

Before they even opened their door, Jon and Karen had done plenty of legwork. They figured out that they wanted to be sole proprietors, as opposed to incorporating or becoming a partnership.

"The city and state you are in can make a difference in how you are viewed and taxed. The direction your business is going in will make a difference, too," Jon says. "In our case, we just want to stay pretty small. If the goal is to be a larger firm, then incorporating may be the way to go."

Also, carefully check out what the tax situation is for businesses in your area. The partners found out, two years into their venture, that they had inadvertently not paid a city/county tax and a transportation tax, neither of which they had ever heard of. Scaring up cash for such a large and unexpected expense can be very damaging to a young company. In addition to taxes, health insurance must be considered.

Also before opening a new office, the Wippichs advise defining one's niche carefully. They tried to be a lot of things to a lot of people in the beginning until they decided that Dotzero should be a high-end studio. Don't take "just-to-pay-the-bills" work unless you want to become known by larger agencies as a place to hand off tedious, uncreative work while they keep the higher-end jobs in-house.

One sort of job that they do occasionally accept is work for charities. Some are able to pay, while others cannot. But all charity clients can help make contacts with new clients who actually do have budgets.

"These projects get your names out there, and they are projects that usually have more freedom attached to them. But do make sure that these are causes that you believe in and get satisfaction out of helping," Karen says.

Day-to-Day Survival

Right away, they designed a complete stationery system so that they looked like the professional designers that they are. They make a conscious effort to attend design-related events and all client meetings in business attire. They "open" the office at the same time every day, even though the business is still in their home. (As business improves, they plan to secure office space elsewhere.)

While Jon was still freelancing, he forced himself to get up and get dressed for work every day by creating a commute for himself: He walked his wife to the bus stop every morning, an eight-block round trip.

"It kept me from lingering over the morning paper or sometimes sleeping in. It really helps to feel and act professional when you are dressed for work and have separated yourself from the house," he says.

These are small, even obvious efforts, Karen says, but you are only playing at being in business if you're not going to take it seriously.

It only took about a month for business to start rolling in at a good pace, and herein lay one of the first surprises for the partners. Even though work was coming in, it wasn't all complete that first month, so no billing could take place, and there was no cash coming in for a while. They learned that partial billing was a good thing: Even after jobs are done, it can still take a month or more to get paid.

In the meantime, a new business's financial needs are many. Early on, the partners found that they needed to outfit a new computer with new software, a $4,000 bite out of the monies they had carefully saved before they opened Dotzero's doors. Maintenance on the computers takes plenty of time and cash, as does keeping up with technology.

So while it may seem like you are billing much more per hour than what you earned for an employer—$100 per hour as opposed to $40 per hour—it doesn't go very far, Karen warns.

Also be ready to handle the administration of the business. Even with Jon and Karen as the business's only employees, between billing, talking with photographers and printers, meeting with clients and finding new business, less and less time is available for design. Even taking time to organize your office and purchase supplies eats away at your day.

"I try to do the same jobs at the same time every week. Say we are trying to find new business: We will look at the schedule and say, 'Let's concentrate on this for a half-day here.' Otherwise, office chores can be very hit and miss," Jon explains.

Know Oneself

A lot of the success and pleasure in running a small office is in knowing yourself. This means acknowledging your strong and weak points, as well as those of your partner, if you have one. Sometimes a weaker area will need to be improved, and sometimes that part of the business can be handed off to someone else—a professional accountant, for instance.

If both partners are weak in a certain area—neither of the Wippichs were crazy about handling the business end—someone will have to step up and get educated. "Force yourself into the role," Karen says. "Jon does this for us now, and he does a really good job, although I know he doesn't enjoy it all that much."

Know, too, what types of clients are best for you, says Jon. The best fit for clients (so far) seems to be small companies that need help from the very start: They need an identity and everything to which it would be applied. Ad agencies with no in-house design departments or that have more work than they can handle have also turned out to be ideal clients.

Finally, Karen Wippich advises anyone on the cusp of going out on his or her own to not fear failure. Acknowledge that failure is a possibility and then move past it.

"There are plenty of very famous, very wealthy business people who have claimed bankruptcy several times in their careers," she says. "But that didn't stop them. People are going to tell you that you can't do this, but if you have a good plan, there's no reason that you can't."

Part Five:

RETHINKING

Section 11: Recovering from the Loss of a Significant Client

The External Big Hit

It's painful but true: The moment a new client is signed on, the end of the relationship has begun. It's a seemingly irreparable hole in the designer's bucket, one that eats up endless hours of new business development and angst.

Obviously, prevention is the best medicine. But is it possible to convince a client to stay? Is it always worth it? What happens when a major client does walk, despite your best efforts?

LIPPA PEARCE DESIGN

How to Be Irreplaceable

The designers at Lippa Pearce Design have discovered that the best way to avoid the heartache and headache of losing a client is to partner with the client so closely that their services are not easily replaceable. But that means that they have to feel in their hearts that a client is indeed a good fit as a partner. Sometimes it means turning work away.

Principal Domenic Lippa, with nearly twenty years of experience as a designer and creative director, has seen his share of clients come and go. Partnering, he says, keeps clients feeling cared for and prevents them from wandering.

Lippa Pearce Design has existed for twelve years, and some of its clients have been with the London-based firm the entire time. They have bucked the belief that most clients will only stay with a design firm for four or five years. But these achievements have not been without the investment of plenty of time and energy in delivering design that will not give clients a reason to look elsewhere.

But at the same time, principal Domenic Lippa feels that it is healthy to imagine that clients might move on at any time. "The fear that they might walk keeps us fresh. Each new job we take on is treated with the same respect and excitement," he says.

Chemistry between personalities is just as important as good design, Lippa believes. So they keep their clients quite close. For example, when a new client comes on board, the size and structure of Lippa Pearce—only eighteen people work there—does not permit him or her to be loaded off on a junior designer. The principals always maintain a direct relationship with all clients. "We let them know that they are as important to us as we are important to them," Lippa adds.

Gauging Relationships

When Lippa Pearce first began doing business, it had some difficult relationships with a handful of clients, Domenic Lippa recalls. The fit between what the client needed and what the design firm could provide was not as tight as it should have been. Over time, Lippa and his partners, Harry Pearce and Giles Calver, had to admit to themselves that they couldn't do everything. The positive side of that judgment was that they could do very good work for certain types of clients.

"We can tell within the first half-hour of meeting a client if we can do business with him," the creative director says. "But my heart still sinks when the chemistry isn't quite there. Still, you have to have integrity and be incredibly honest."

A very transparent relationship with current and prospective clients alike goes a long way toward keeping people on board. It consistently sells the value of design, so that clients appreciate and understand the work that they do.

When Clients Leave

Of course, it is demoralizing when a client chooses to leave, and there are always commercial pressures to stay profitable. But it's the same as with any situation in life, Lippa says: Sometimes you just have to accept it. There is usually nothing a design firm can do to make the customer stay.

"You just have to motivate yourself the next day and say, "I have one less client. But I have others that I am equally enthusiastic about," Lippa says.

The situation is often harder on staff members, especially younger designers. They don't see the politics of it; instead, they take the news as a personal slap at their work or talent. Lippa tries to make them understand that the departure is exactly the same situation as having a great idea that a client doesn't go with. There is a lot of subjectivity involved.

"But it's so important to remember that design is a part of life: It is not all of life," he says.

To help everyone maintain perspective, whether clients are coming or going, Lippa Pearce takes on plenty of work for human rights organizations and other issue-based groups. These are jobs that feed the soul of the designer.

"The work is a reminder that what we do is not as important as someone losing their life," Lippa says.

Who's Right, Who's Wrong

Clients usually base their financial and manufacturing decisions on fact: hard data that supports what they must do. But design is full of intuition: Every finished project can potentially be judged right or wrong; it depends on who is making the call.

Lippa knows that some designers have made a very successful living by telling their clients, "This is the right design for you. Take it or leave it."

Lippa Pearce does not take that tack. Instead, its designers concentrate on understanding the client's problem. Doing their homework isn't the prettiest part of a design project, but it is as important (if not more) than actually rendering an on-paper solution.

"Coming up with a solution is the easy part: There are 100 possible solutions floating about out there. Understanding the problem is the hard part," Lippa points out.

They see themselves as partners to their clients, not suppliers. Lippa wants their customers to feel as though they can ring up and talk to him about creative problems anytime. We're all in this together, he says.

They are also encouraged by the fact that, within the graphic design industry today, friendships tend to be real and healthy, not secretive or aggressive as in days past. One design firm might even suggest another to a client as that job walks out the door.

"We all used to feel that everyone else is doing everything better, but then you discover that they have problems, too, just different from ours," Lippa says.

Whether they are dealing with fellow designers or clients, Lippa Pearce designers try to maintain perspective. Rejection, on a professional level, is rarely personal, even when "it rips your heart out," the designer says.

"We all have families and try to get home and enjoy ourselves. We don't want the business to overtake us. You have to be philosophical about it all," he says.

COLBY & PARTNERS

Deal with It and Move On

It seems as though, in the universe of advertising agencies, clients are more fickle, hiring and firing their outside marketing support as the winds change direction. So it makes sense to speak with an advertising professional with many years of experience and perhaps a more measured look at the sometimes unpleasant, sometimes disastrous occasion when a client leaves.

Rick Colby is just such a professional. No less than three agencies have carried his name as part of their moniker in the past seventeen years, and he has worked with clients as diverse as Suzuki and California Avocados. Losing a client is never fun, he admits, but Colby tries to maintain a healthy outlook for himself and his office when it does happen.

Advertising giant Jay Chiat was quoted as saying that you start losing a client the moment you get it. It's a dictum that— unfortunately—is as true in advertising as it is in graphic design. The very day a new account is brought on board, that client's eye begins to wander: Is there a better agency for me out there? And other design firms are always circling in the surrounding waters, waiting for that first drop of blood that marks a tear in the relationship.

Rick Colby, principal of five-year-old Colby & Partners, Santa Monica, California, estimates that he has served approximately one hundred clients in his years as an ad agency creative director and partner. He also estimates that, if even an unfounded rumor gets out that an agency client is unhappy, that client will get 70 to 150 packages from competing ad firms in the next several days.

"If there is a crack in the armor," he says, "you are dead."

Colby is a realist. He doesn't take things personally. He knows that you can never stop pitching new business and that you can't rely on anything but yourself and your staff. Clients are just too fluid these days.

Selecting Clients

It's possible to lessen the chances of losing a client and suffering the resulting heartache by selecting the right clients in the first place.

Colby says that over the years, he has taken on clients for a number of reasons: the opportunity to do great work, earn good money, or enter a new category of business. Some clients are taken on for a period of observation: They just might develop into something profitable—or not.

"We would take on accounts like that and not make any money— we accepted them based on what might develop later on. These days I am very reluctant to do that," Colby says. "I have learned the hard way that you don't have to make a lot of money or even a profit, but you can't lose money."

The slide into unprofitability is the beginning of the end of a relationship with a client. Hours spent on the account have to be restricted, the client senses that there is trouble afoot, and that business is gone.

The agency principal also prefers that no client, no matter how attractive or lucrative, represent any more than 50 percent of his business. That way, if the largest client goes, the agency won't go with it. Also, keeping a balance amongst clients is better from a creative standpoint: In so doing, morale and creativity are kept healthy.

But this can be perversely difficult, particularly if Colby's agency is doing its job well. With the proper marketing, the client grows, becoming more and more dominant on the agency job list. Then, a painfully familiar scenario can develop: If a campaign is very successful, the client's marketing director begins to attract attention, is hired away by another company, and a new marketing director comes in. The new director wants to work with his or her own people, and the ad agency or design firm that made it all possible is fired.

"It's a stupid thing for a client to do, but it happens all the time," Colby says.

To keep a client happy, find out what he or she wants, then "plus it" somehow. A design or ad agency must do better than the client could do itself. And pay attention to exactly what a client wants: Some need a partner and full service; others just want creative or strategic thinking. Give them what they want.

When Disaster Strikes

A huge part of the client/agency relationship is personal chemistry, but when the client leaves, Colby warns against taking the split personally—even if it is personal. As commander of the troops, allowing any break to sink further than skin deep can cause you to become depressed. Dejection quickly communicates itself to staff.

"I learned this from one of the partners of an agency I worked at: Go ahead and be depressed for a few hours. But the next day, you better come in bouncing down the hallway and talking about all of the great things that are going to happen next. Everyone else is going to be depressed, so you have to recover or else you will never get out of the hole. You have to get everyone else looking toward the future again," he says. "If for no other reason, recover for the other people in the company."

Try to let the staff know what the problem was, particularly if the break was for the best: Perhaps the client wasn't a good fit for the company, or that the client itself is having financial problems.

Of course, sometimes when a client leaves, morale isn't the only thing hurting. If the agency's financial situation is affected, Colby feels the kindest thing to do is to quickly let people go and make other necessary cuts. Some agencies will string out this process, hoping for a miracle, but in the end, the outcome is the same. Nobody—not the fired or the ones who get to stay—wants to work for a bankrupt company.

Damage Control

The best thing to do from a staff standpoint is to get everyone excited about new business activity. Get a new pitch in motion, and involve everyone.

Should a client's departure be explained to other clients, just to calm their nerves? If it is a small client, Colby's company won't say anything. But if it is a really big client, he will go to the other clients and explain what happened. "I will tell them that we are fine and minimize any affect this had on the company. Otherwise, your remaining clients can get very nervous, and other agencies will begin swarming around."

Colby does not mean to paint a dire picture, full of dread. But a little fear is a good thing: It keeps you on your toes, he says. Be attentive but not paralyzed, and never, never get complacent.

KMS TEAM

On Being Prepared

It almost sounds impossible, but for almost two decades, KMS Team, a fifty-person design firm based in Munich, Germany, never unintentionally lost a client. It was a record of which the firm was proud. Then in late 2001, the inevitable happened. Two significant clients were gone.

These hits were significant, but KMS was not unprepared. Executive partner Christoph Rohrer explains what has happened to his company since, as well as what they have done to prevent future losses.

The loss of a significant client is something every design firm dreads, and for fifteen years, KMS Team dodged the bullet. But two events in September 2001—surprisingly, not related to September 11— led to the loss of two large clients.

The company had been working for the ProSiebenSat.1 Group, one of the major German private television broadcast organizations. KMS had accompanied the previous merger between ProSieben and Sat.1, developed the identity of the new holding, and were in the process of defining the identity system and communications for the group's subsidiary companies. But in September, Kirch Media AG, the major shareholder of ProSiebenSat.1, unexpectedly announced their merger with the main company. The result was a sudden cessation of all running jobs.

The second incident followed not long after. For the past five years, KMS had been doing the international motor shows for Audi in Frankfurt, Geneva, Paris, Detroit, and Tokyo. But beginning in 2001, a number of management changes took place at Audi, and it soon became clear that KMS's and Audi's opinions differed. So in September, the client and design firm mutually agreed to discontinue their long-term partnership.

Both of these incidents sent nervous shivers through KMS. But it made the firm's principals take note of what they were doing right and what they could do to prevent shake-ups like this in the future.

Why Clients Leave

The most painful reason for a client to leave is when he or she is not satisfied with the work a design firm is doing.

"Since we never consciously do 'bad' work for a client, it is mostly a question of how different people judge results differently," Rohrer explains. This is especially the case in large companies with highly hierarchical structures and various decision-makers at different levels. This leads to subjective calls about your work.

Politics are difficult to fight, but if you are looking at the client's company as a whole and anticipating influences from other departments, you should at least have some warning when the mood might be souring, Rohrer advises. Also, stay in contact with the real decision makers.

Clients also go away when they run out of money, which is an especially dangerous situation. Not only does the design firm lose a client, but it might also never recover costs or charges for work already done. Keep your eyes on the economic and personnel situation of your clients, and whether things look bright or dim, get advance payments and bill as soon as possible after a job is finished, Rohrer says. For long-term projects, define and bill separate phases or on a monthly basis.

Finally, companies can merge or be bought out in the blink of an eye, which usually leads to personnel changes. The only way your account will survive if your contact person does not is to be certain you have created very solid relationships with others within the company in addition to your main contact.

Be Prepared

Rohrer recommends distribution of risk as the best possible preparation for and prevention of disaster, citing these specific methods:

- Keep your client portfolio balanced. The loss of your biggest client should not endanger the entire studio.
- If a large client does leave, consider replacing it with two smaller ones. They may not pay as well, but they can be a lot more fun, which is good for morale. But be aware, Rohrer says, that this option will influence the way the studio is structured: Big clients and complex projects need big teams and lots of organization. Smaller clients need small, tight teams.
- Work for clients in different commercial fields, Rohrer recommends. This reduces the risk of a domino effect when one field of business goes down.
- Try to find new clients in emerging or growing markets, which widens your horizon of experience and your ability to advise existing clients.
- Diversify your services. When clients run out of money, they cut advertising budgets. But they will still have to present at important trade shows and they will definitely have to do an annual report.
- Be financially conservative: Don't take all of the money out of the company or rely solely on credit or outside financing. When the economy is difficult, the banks won't be nearly as friendly as they are in good times.

- Stay flexible. If you lose a big client, you will have to cut costs quickly. This usually translates to laying off employees. Keep their periods of notice short and find other ways to work (such as with freelancers).
- Keep your PR efforts in motion. Enter awards shows: They won't land you new clients, but winning the odd award will definitely boost morale.

Recovery Period

Rohrer is philosophical when it comes to handling the aftermath of a client loss. "The goal of a good designer is to do good design. If that is not possible with a specific client, you may save your energy for somebody else," he says.

Of course, you may find yourself in a serious financial situation. You won't sleep at night, and you will worry a lot about the future. But this should also cause you to sit up and start fighting.

"Rely on the people around you: your partners, your employees, your friends and family. They can help you. Listen to them," Rohrer says. It's no good to sit down and cry. ""Other mothers have beautiful daughters, too'—that's a German saying. The only thing that will help is to go out and do great projects for somebody else."

The recovery period is also the right time to reevaluate what you might do differently in the future. What can you do to keep clients? Foremost, remember who is in charge of the relationship.

"You may be a nice guy, you may go out for a beer with your clients, you may give them discounts, you may help them with their internal presentations, you may send them nice Christmas cards and win tons of awards. But they pay you for the work you do for them. If they are satisfied with that work, they probably won't leave," Rohrer says.

But that does not mean to obediently fork over exactly what the client anticipates. Sometimes the best solution is not the one the client had in mind. Try to exhibit a different point of view that causes him to rethink his or her briefing and to make more difficult decisions. Rohrer also insists on being demanding.

"This will change your position from an exchangeable service provider to a valuable consultant," he says.

Remember that you are solving the client's problems, not your own. The closer you listen and the more you know about a client's situation and objectives, the better your solutions will be. Look at the company as a whole, not as the single department you work with. KMS designers call this "tiefendesign," or depth design.

Today, KMS Team has replaced both of the clients it lost in 2001 with equal or even more interesting clients. Rohrer says that, looking back, his group benefited from what was an initial shock.

"We grew even stronger for the future," he says.

KENDRA POWER DESIGN & COMMUNICATION, INC.

Learning from Loss

Even when they are being provided with excellent creative, clients occasionally walk. In-house contacts can change; supervisors may force their creative staff to buy design by low bid; or perhaps a client hires its own in-house staff. But in every loss there is a lesson, says Kathy Kendra, partner with Mark Power in Kendra Power Design & Communication, Pittsburgh, Pennsylvania.

When she began her career, Kendra's focus was solely on design. Over time, she has also learned the importance of establishing and maintaining client relationships—even, in some cases, with clients who have decided to leave.

It is as important to know how to manage a client's expectations as it is to manage the creative development of a project, says Kathy Kendra. To keep clients happy, she, her partner Mark Power, and their staff must be able to competently bounce in and out of creative and project management roles.

"Good project management can help a good project achieve greater success," Kendra says.

She has learned that all aspects of a project should be thought of in the same way that the creative portion is: If the creative meets the goals and objectives of the client, it will prove to be a greater success if all other aspects of the project have been thoroughly managed, including the schedule, budget, and delivery. Genuine interest must be displayed.

That interest begins at the very first client meeting. "Share in the excitement of the presentation—be enthusiastic," Kendra says. "Find their burden in the assignment and lessen it. [Maybe it is to] develop the schedule or handle the delivery—take their hot button on as your own and handle it. Make yourself a valued member of their team."

To keep clients on board, it's crucial to show them that you are as invested in the ultimate success of the project as they are. Even better, listen to their objectives and improve on them in some way, always looking for a way to give them a bonus: Perhaps the piece can be produced at less cost or delivery can be pushed to come in ahead of schedule.

Departure Prevention

A solid relationship is the best vaccine to guard against losing a valuable client. That begins by figuring out, before a job is even accepted, if a potential client is a good fit for Kendra's office.

"Any new client or project opportunity is first discussed with the entire staff to determine if it is a valid 'partner' to consider," Kendra says. They evaluate new client relationships on 1) creative opportunity, 2) financial opportunity, and 3) whether the client will be an enjoyable or interesting one with which to work. "If a new opportunity is able to satisfy two of the three, we will establish the relationship."

Kendra and Power are also particularly mindful of shifts in the markets, watching for opportunities to appear or disappear. When new opportunities present themselves, they try to match them with the creative preferences of their staff in order to maintain enthusiasm amongst their designers, not just bring in new work.

Finally, when a job has been accepted by her team, Kendra encourages her designers to enjoy the creative development process as much as possible, when the enthusiasm and love of the craft is still fresh.

"This is the part of the process where the client has not had a chance to critique it," she says. In this way, even if everything goes awry later, her designers have a chance to have a positive feeling about every project.

She encourages her designers to be emotional about the work, and on some jobs, even to fall in love with the project to the point where they truly want their creative output to be selected as "the one." But the partners decide beforehand which of the projects have this star potential and allow their team to spend more time and emotional investment on these.

Damage Control

When a client does choose to go, Kendra first tries to determine why the account was lost. Did they offer a less than ideal solution? Was there a scheduling problem or a budget surprise? Where and how did the communication breakdown occur? If the relationship had otherwise been successful up until that point, she will approach the client directly and discuss why the relationship ended.

Then the principal can do a studio self-analysis to determine if all of the components of her studio were working properly. Perhaps critical procedures aren't being followed or certain members of staff are feeling uninspired. She will check out her office's technology to make sure it is up to snuff. "Basically, I am looking for any chinks in the armor that may have helped to cause the lost relationship," she says.

To keep staff spirits up, the partners always keep an honest, open relationship with their employees, being forthright about the events that lead to a lost relationship. She also stresses looking for the silver lining—that is, it is an excellent opportunity to improve the entire machine. The partners also constantly remind staff about their successes, especially in the face of such failures.

Kendra also maintains relationships even when they turn inactive by keeping clients' contact names on her mailing list and by offering assistance to the client's in-house staff if they should become overloaded. "[We will] take on any project to help them, regardless of size," she says.

Her company keeps all clients, past and present, aware of any changes in the studio regarding staff and capabilities, as well as the completion of any noteworthy projects that would be pertinent to them.

Kendra and Power know that every client relationship will not be endless, no matter how exceptional the efforts of their team might be. The association they have with clients is highly analogous to the creative process. The end result may not turn out exactly how they envisioned, but it's always worthwhile to look back at their process to see what they did right.

"Find a success, no matter how small, in each project," Kendra insists.

Section 12: Recovering from the Loss of a Significant Creative

The Internal Big Hit

In some ways, design firm principals take the loss of a significant member of staff harder than they do the loss of a client. It feels more personal: Endless hours have gone into that person's hiring, training, nurturing, and support. To lose him or her can be like becoming estranged from a family member.

Four completely disparate situations are described in the following section. One firm works extremely hard to keep employees happy; another puts equal focus on training and on making staff feel integral to the firm's success. Yet another office focuses on being prepared for inevitable departures. And finally, when something that one is totally unprepared for happens—in this case, the events of September 11, 2001—how a business can survive the departure of almost two-thirds of its staff.

EM2 DESIGN

Making Staff Feel Completely at Home

Word on the streets of Decatur, Georgia, is that EM2 is a good place to work. The thirteen-year-old design firm is very democratic in its structure, and turnover is low. Its offices are a pleasure to work in. Any troubles that arise are dealt with quickly and are not allowed to fester.

Principal Chris Martin's success in creating a terrific atmosphere in which to work is signaled by the fact that he has never had an employee up and leave in a huff. And the few that have left over the years, although they have been missed, have done so graciously and without hard feelings.

The culture of EM2 is an exception in the design world: Most employees have been with the company for five years or more, and turnover is low. But because it is a small firm—made up of just ten people—it must always be wary of the departure of any person: The impact is dramatic even if it is infrequent. Of the employees who have left over the years, Martin has tried to gather lessons.

The first was a very valuable and talented staff member who was a big personality and contributor in the studio.

"He wanted to pursue more in the technology and Web site disciplines and had learned all he could from our company. When he left to join a much larger Web development firm, we all felt the shift," Martin says. This was a case where everyone was sad to see the person go, but the departure was a natural and unavoidable evolution.

The silver lining in this story is that after about two years of working with the new employer and some shifts in that company's culture, the employee decided to come back to EM2. "We were serious when we told him he would always have a place on our team if he ever wanted it," Martin says.

Another situation involved two very talented employees, each brought into the fold about a month apart. The unique thing about these employees is that they were both hired away from the same design agency. Therefore, they entered the EM2 culture with somewhat preconceived notions about what the environment would be like based on their experiences at their previous employer. After about a year, it became apparent that neither employee was happy.

"My partner and I talked about it with both employees and acknowledged that it didn't seem to a fit. We encouraged them to find what was truly right for them," Martin recalls.

As it turned out, one employee soon began freelance writing and now works with EM2 on a contract basis. The other person landed a job in Europe that was an ideal fit for him.

"I believe that there is a perfect fit for everyone," Martin says. "But you have to tell the truth and be fearless when it comes to change."

The final example is one of a poor fit and poor skills combined. An individual was hired to do new business development, and after nine months had not produced any prospects. After Martin discovered that the employee also had a very chauvinistic attitude toward female members of staff, he was terminated almost immediately.

"This incident occurred very early in the evolution of our business when I was green in regard to HR responsibilities. I think had I had more experience in hiring and managing people, I would have seen the red flags long before hiring this person," Martin says.

The three stories point out three different reasons people leave a company: An individual "grows out of" what used to be a good fit; an individual is a good skill-set fit, but not a good cultural fit; or a person just doesn't fit in at all. Each scenario is one that firm principals should be watching for on their radar screens constantly, Martin says.

Prevent, Don't Patch

It's much easier to keep employees than it is to find new ones, Martin knows. So he and his partner Maxey Andress have built a company with a very flat structure in which everyone has a major role in making the company run properly. In essence, each person is a vital, senior member of staff. Without each person doing his or her own job properly, the machine does not hum as it should. In addition, an open-door policy encourages employees to bring problems to the principals right away.

"There is a true democracy here, which can be a detriment at times. Great work can come out of a dictatorship—the 'my way or the highway' approach to management—where there is one person leading the vision, but it seems turnover is very high at agencies where that is practiced," Martin says.

Another factor that keeps attrition low is that the principals share financial information with their employees at quarterly meetings. And employees are very interested in the company's progress because its profit-sharing plan is very generous when times are good.

"When the company is profitable, we share that profit with our employees. So they have a genuine interest in how sales are going and what new accounts we are mining," Martin says.

Other factors that increase the "staying power" of critical members of staff:

- The company tries to be flexible about time off. If someone needs an afternoon off or asks to work at home during an extended maternity leave, the partners try to be accommodating.
- The company just purchased a big, old house on the outskirts of Decatur that very much fits the culture of the company. The place has been transformed from a home into a working office, but Martin notes that it is still very

comfortable. "It has a huge front porch that is great for brainstorming meetings," he adds.

• Acceptance of projects that requires their staff to put in a lot of overtime are a group decision. There are also no all-nighters, and they frown on people working past 7:00 or 8:00 P.M. The company has turned down some rather lucrative projects, but that's all part of showing employees that the company's beliefs are not just lip service.

Martin says that, even though his staff and their families are very close and spend a lot of social time together, they are not a family.

"I don't want to be dad. I say we are a community of people. I've even gone beyond that recently to say we are like a tribe. Some of what I have read about Indian tribes and how they function is ideal: Everyone has an important job, yet the group is small. It is a very interdependent type of structure," the principal explains.

Choose Challenges Carefully

People are choosing their challenges very carefully these days, says Martin, and they are often basing their choices on lifestyle factors. He wants to help his people live the best, most humane lives possible.

Design is a very emotional industry. Creativity is a very spiritual activity. The human element cannot be avoided. Everyone at EM2 is fairly spiritual, not necessarily in the religious sense, but in a metaphysical sense. So a healthy, intertwined approach to life works well for them.

"You are reaching in and you don't know what will come forth. A stressful environment does not support the best outcomes. Design is an activity that must be nurtured—that's how the best work comes forth," Martin says.

THE RICHARDS GROUP
When to Hold On and When to Let Go

The Richards Group has quietly, impressively produced effective, award-winning design for forty-five years. During that time, Stan Richards' knack for selecting extremely talented designers has become legendary. Many of the people he has brought on board stay for many years. And among the group that decides to strike out on their own are a veritable "who's who" of design practitioners.

In a way, Richards gets the best of both worlds: In-house, he creates an environment that inspires people to do their very best. If those people should decide to go, they carry his lessons with them and can succeed anywhere.

Design firm founder Jack Summerford. Pentagram's Woody Pirtle. Wieden & Kennedy's creative director Hal Curtis. Houston designer Jerry Herring, and the internationally acclaimed John Norman. What do they have in common? All are alumni of The Richards Group of Dallas. It's an exceptional list of talents to come from a single agency.

Managing principal Dick Mitchell. Principals Brian Boyd, Steve Miller, Lewis Acevedo, Robin Ayres, Horacio Cobos, and Tom Nynas. What's the common thread here? All are in-house professionals still employed by The Richards Group—lesser-known in press circles perhaps, but certainly all people of exceptional talent and drive. What's more, their combined years of employment at the firm totals an amazing 125 years.

"The interesting thing is that there is little difference between the people who have left and had great success and those who have stayed and had great success," says Richards, principal of the 520-person firm. "They were all hired because they were very talented and a good fit for this organization. Those characteristics are universal to our design group, and they are what make people a success if they should decide to leave."

Citing a specific instance, Richards notes that Woody Pirtle could easily have stayed with his group and been eminently successful. "He is a really good guy, and he has great communication skills," he explains. "Now take Dick Mitchell, who heads up our design unit and who has been with us for about twenty-five years. He has those same skills, but he has built a powerful career from within the company."

Finding the Right People

Spotting talent is easy, Richards says: It shows in a designer's book. A good work ethic isn't quite so evident, but it will reveal itself as that person works side-by-side with others. Richards' designers often are focused on their work for fourteen to sixteen hours per day. It takes a special determination to do that year after year, he notes. There has to be the commitment to spend whatever time is necessary to finesse details that no one else will notice.

Another requirement for working at The Richards Group: No arrogance. "Arrogance is not uncommon among ad people and designers. There is no place for it here," the agency owner says. "Here there is a strong commitment to respecting each other, whether it is someone in the mail room or our most senior designer. We have the same commitment to respect our clients as well."

Talent (and being willing to use it), a strong work ethic, and respect for others: These are all things that stand people in good stead throughout their careers, Richards notes, whether they are working for him or not.

Encouraging Longevity

To encourage good people to stay with his company, Richards has a simple plan: He tries to provide no incentive for them to leave. He makes certain that people are compensated as well as they would be elsewhere, and he works hard to create an environment where there is a chance to do good work all day, every day.

"I also give them the opportunity to manage their own relationships with clients so that they are in control of that relationship. I also make sure that they have the resources they need in order to produce good work and that they don't have to spend an enormous amount of time dealing with the business side of the business," he says.

Most people who leave firms go not because they want more money, but because they want more respect, he believes. He and his managers treat employees like the grown-ups they are, not like children who need to be coddled. That means they must be respected as valuable team members. In addition, he must respect an employee's choice to leave and pursue his or her own destiny.

Of course, Richards is always sorry to see people go, but he does want the transition to be as easy as possible for that person and his or her co-workers.

"We want people to go away as friends and to become a long-term cohort of the agency. In future years, there may be ways we can help each other and be supportive," he says, adding that quite often his company has what he calls "boomerangs." "People leave here, and for whatever reason, some decide to come back."

Some firms drive people away simply through poor business practice, he adds. They don't keep accurate timesheets, for instance, which means they don't bill properly or enough, which in turn means they can't operate profitably enough to reward people properly. Other firms don't charge adequate fees: They may get a lot of work because they are charging the lowest price, he points out, but doing that over an extended period of years will eventually exhaust and discourage employees.

Another major problem some firms have is holding on to people who are not contributing as much as they could or should.

"The secret to long-term success, if there is one, is to keep your best people and identify those people who are not terribly important to the growth of the organization and encourage them to go elsewhere," Richards says.

Replacing Key Staff

The fact is, Richards says, is that you can never truly replace a valuable staff member. No one else will have the specific and wonderful talents that person had. So do the best you can with similar talents within the organization, he says—The Richards Group prefers to hire from within its own walls whenever possible—and elevate that person or persons to new levels of responsibility.

Growing their own talent has proven to be a successful method for The Richards Group. "We get the really bright kids right out of school and bring them in at their first level of their career, and then try to keep them forever," Richards explains. "But if we do lose them, there is always someone behind them, somebody talented and experienced enough to step into their role."

WATERS DESIGN
The Unthinkable and Its Aftermath

On September 11, 2001, John Waters and his staff at Waters Design found themselves with ringside seats to the most horrific scene imaginable. From their offices on the 28th floor of 22 Courtland Street, New York, New York, they watched one plane, and then another smash into buildings that were no more than a football field away from their windows.

They consider themselves fortunate: Everyone escaped from the offices unharmed—physically, at least. But in the ensuing months, life has been extremely difficult. Waters' staff of twenty people has dwindled to six: Some people could not bear coming back to work, and Waters has had to let some people go due to a precipitous drop in business. But recovery has begun.

A news release issued from John Waters on October 4, 2001, retells his firm's experience best.

On the morning of September 11, I was at my desk on the 28th floor, facing out the window directly across the plaza from the World Trade Center, when the first plane hit. In stunned silence, I watched with my colleagues as flames and smoke poured from the building—and then people began to jump. In sheer horror, we looked on, trying to think of what we could do—should do, when the second plane hit. A huge ball of fire, filled with debris, was flying toward us. Instantly, we knew we were under attack and ran for the stairwell.

The good news is that we all got out alive. But we left behind over twenty Web servers, multiple workstations, all of our resource files, our library, and personal effects. Fortunately, we had back-up systems running three times a day, and most of our work was on tapes located off site. By the end of Thursday, two days after the attack, Armando Jimarez, our CTO, had re-established our e-mail network on borrowed servers and placed simple splash pages on the dozen or so Web sites and development sites we had hosted which were now down. On the following Monday we had our first full staff meeting in temporary office space. Without hesitation, everyone agreed that we must continue, regardless of the difficulty, to serve our clients—to survive this disaster, even to excel because of it.

At this writing, John Waters and his staff are still fighting to get back to some semblance of normal. They have relocated to space in the famous Pushpin Building, and their old space has finally come onto the market after extensive repairs: They are not going back. Despite the fact that Waters Design has premium insurance coverage, it has not yet been able to settle its claims. The staff has been reduced from twenty to six people. A firm that usually bills $200,000 a month had no income at all in September, and October wasn't much better. The following seven months have shown gradual increases in billing, but it's still not what it should be.

All that being said, Waters feels fortunate. "There was no loss of life, and no one was hurt," he says simply. "We were the lucky ones."

The first week after the disaster was bedlam. He was able to quickly locate all of his staff members but one, and it was a terrifying day-and-a-half until they were able to speak to communications strategist Karen McCarron. The following Monday, the entire staff met in borrowed office space and unanimously voted to stay in business.

It was a telling moment for them all: Their commitment to clients and each other was stronger than any of them might have suspected before. They set up in their homes and in borrowed spaces, and they tried to stay in constant touch with each other by e-mail.

"There's a great quote, from Luciano De Crescenzo that I think captures our state of mind: 'We are, each of us angels with only one wing, and we can only fly by embracing each other,'" Waters says. "We all had to stay together—psychologically."

Protecting the Team

Waters Design has always had a very tight teamwork approach, even when the firm was at sixty people. Teamwork is a critical part of the design business, the principal believes, and teams require close communication in order to stay vital.

Even with his reduced staff, Waters believes that staying in close contact with everyone is important. Don't hold back information: At weekly staff meetings and other impromptu get-togethers, the Waters Design staff discusses everything—the financial condition of the company, staffing issues, difficulties with clients, personal struggles, and new business ideas. Everyone is encouraged to speak up and put their problems or difficulties on the table.

"You can't solve a problem unless you know about it," Waters says, "and the more people who know about it, the more likely it is you can find the best solution."

He and his wife/partner and creative director Cheryl Oppenheim Waters are also observing people carefully now, watching for signs of fragility before someone reaches a breaking point. Their office policy has always been that if someone works late one day, as long as his commitments to others have been met, he can take time off the next day. Lenient provisions like this are even more important now, Waters says.

Another already-existing office perk is a summer schedule: The office is closed on Fridays, and the staff works from 8:30 A.M. to 6 P.M. Monday through Thursday. The partners initially thought that they would have to cancel the reduced schedule—they fully expect business to be getting heavier in the summer—but if there was any year that it would be important, it was 2002. It's crucial for people to have time off now, Waters says.

Sometimes everyone needs a break in the middle of the day, he adds. "In the past few months, we will say to everyone, 'Stop—let's go out and all have lunch together. Let's forget about things for a few hours.' It does really help."

Things are looking up at Waters Design: Business is starting to come back. In fact, the firm posted two new job opportunities on its Web site at this writing, and interviews had begun. Waters and his partner are looking for a different sort of person now. An impressive résumé is less important than is someone with a healthy mindset.

"We are examining their outlook on life and how they deal with people. Those things are so much more important," Waters points out. When in doubt about whether or not to hire someone, go with your gut, he says. "If I have a funny feeling about somebody, no matter how wonderful or grandiose their résumé or recommendations are, invariably, I will have made a wrong decision if I hire them."

Waters knows that life and work will never be the same again. He and his employees will continue to struggle and must continue to accommodate each other whenever necessary. One designer just left the firm to take the summer off and get away from it all.

"I hate to lose him and hope he comes back," Waters says. "We have had several sessions in the office where people are in tears, just talking and reviewing what happened. We have also had some funny moments and a fair amount of laughter. Laughter is very important. The one thing that we are all aware of now is how lucky we are."

Looking Ahead

It's the nature of a team to want to win or at least excel, and Waters plans to give his team as many chances to do well as he can. One way to do this is to provide an opportunity to contribute new ideas to the business.

"Most designers are filled with ideas and really want to contribute," he says. "Often they don't know they can make suggestions or they don't know how to implement their ideas."

It's the manager's job to show them the way. For instance, in November 2001, in a discussion about the anthrax scare and the apprehension many people were experiencing about the previously innocuous mail, someone suggested producing e-greeting cards for clients and friends. Virtual mail was safe, and it spread cheer amid all the gloom. With Waters' encouragement, the staff took the idea further. In two weeks, Cheryl and designers Phillip Lockwood-Holmes and Jennifer Sterling put together a pricing model, a schedule, designed four sample cards, and designed and launched the Web site Custom iCards.biz.

Two of the sample cards were sold immediately from the site, and half a dozen others were custom designed for clients before the end of the year. It was exciting, enjoyable work, Waters says, and the firm even made a little money.

Since that time, the idea has expanded.

"We are now developing Custom iSpots, interactive online commercials which are delivered via e-mail to a target audience. It's Web site will launch this summer. All of the staff feels a certain pride in ownership in these business ideas," Waters says. "They realize that these new initiatives are keeping us alive."

BAILEY LAUERMAN

Preparation and Prevention

Jim Lauerman, principal with Rich Bailey of Bailey Lauerman, Lincoln, Nebraska, estimates that it costs 160 percent of an employee's salary to replace him or her. Add to that the emotional costs as well as the hassle factor to a company, and the logic in keeping employees happy and at their desks is underscored many times over.

Lauerman's firm, now at seventy people, is bound to have employees coming and going no matter what. But the office partners and their senior management have a number of concrete efforts in motion that they hope will keep departures to a minimum. Good staff members are just too valuable a resource to squander.

Nobody likes to think of a significant creative member of staff leaving, says Jim Lauerman, principal of Bailey Lauerman, Lincoln, Nebraska. But everyone knows it is going to happen sooner or later. And one thing is for certain: The timing is never good.

"A while back, we had two very key people in our creative department who walked in at 8:15 in the morning, resigned, and left immediately to start their own office. We had an 8:30 A.M. meeting with a client—a meeting that involved both of them," he recalls. That was definitely not an enjoyable day, he adds.

Because of the normal ebb and flow of the design business, agency owners often find that they have too many projects and not enough (at least, qualified) designers. Sometimes, designers are sitting idle with no jobs to work on. Add to that mix free will—creative staff can walk out at any time, sometimes to become your competition—and it's a wonder that studios ever achieve the right balance between work and staff.

Preventive Measures

Bailey Lauerman, in its thirty-two years of existence, has developed a number of stop-gaps designed for pre-damage control. The significance of these measures becomes apparent if a key member of staff does leave: Hopefully, not even a ripple will be felt by the firm's clients.

First of all, Lauerman, partner Bailey, and other members of senior staff always work directly with the company's top fifteen clients. They contribute to the ongoing relationship in tandem with other senior creative staff. In this way, even if several senior members left the firm, the principals still have a firm handhold on what is going on with the accounts.

Second, Bailey Lauerman workers are required to sign a non-competition agreement upon hire, and they must now give thirty-days' notice prior to leaving: Lauerman doesn't want any more surprises. A human resources person monitors the progress and overall happiness of every employee. She is always checking to make certain that staff feels included and a vital part of the overall success of the company.

What they are trying to avoid is what Lauerman calls an "island employee." These people won't go out to lunch with other employees, they don't take part in in-office events, and although they go through the motions of their work, they don't seem completely engaged.

"We don't want those people to float away," he says. "I have always felt that replacing someone is like taking on one more very large client. You have to network and recruit and interview. In addition, you have to take on that person's work until he is replaced."

Lauerman says that management accepts the blame when people, especially top talent, walk. Perhaps they felt that they were not getting enough recognition or autonomy—things that his company can easily provide if it is paying attention. The company's management bears the responsibility if people are unhappy for legitimate reasons, he adds.

So each member of senior management, together with the human resources manager, checks in with employees periodically. The company also awards individual and team-wide bonuses when possible; it keeps employees up-to-date on how the company is doing; and it includes top performers on key and non-key decisions. Lauerman and Bailey also try to extend small but meaningful gestures, such as inviting a designer to attend a dinner meeting with a client. It's a lot of extra work, given the number of employees they must monitor, but well worth the effort.

Still, the president says, they could do better.

"We can never work hard enough on keeping the star performers. And it's too easy to spend way too much time rectifying and correcting the less than acceptable performance of low performers, should we find that to be the case. In the meantime, by focusing on the problems, we are failing to recognize those that are doing the best work," Lauerman says, noting that when a top performer walks out the door, it can cause a very nasty domino effect. "These people are influential wherever they go, so they may be able to drag even more people away from our firm."

The Recovery Period

Even with all of these efforts, senior creative members of staff do leave. It's tough, says Lauerman, even after more than three decades in the business.

"We call it the hangover period. It still puts me in a funk. When a client leaves, I take it personally. When an employee leaves, it's just the same," he says, adding that he can't allow himself to wallow. "I kick myself to get out of the blues, then very quickly meet with other staffers to let them know what happened. I tell them what I really mean: that we hate to see them go, but that we wish them well. You have to be really careful here because you will get people in an even bigger funk if their BS detectors go off and they don't think you are telling them the truth. You have to remember that there will be stories floating around that can cause damage, and the people who leave will have their own versions."

Then in another month or so, Lauerman or his partner will get back in front of the staff and once again reinforce that the company is still viable and continuing to move forward. Then it's right back to reinforcing good performance whenever possible. Even people who have only been with the company for a year or two are liable to snag a compliment from one of the principals or be told that their efforts are making a difference.

They have to know they are appreciated, Lauerman concludes, or they will go elsewhere to get that satisfaction.

Section 13: Setting a New Direction
Filing a Revised Flight Plan with Clients and Staff

There comes a time for every design firm when change is inevitable: The business must increase or decrease in size. New categories of work develop; old ones fade away. And sometimes, there's a dream that absolutely must be pursued.

How do you make your clients and staff understand these changes? Is it possible to get these changes in motion without harming the core of the original company? Whether a firm is moving to a new space, developing a new line of business, reiterating to clients what makes it special, or completely reinventing itself, setting off in a new direction presents many challenges.

KINETIK COMMUNICATION GRAPHICS/KITCHEN [K]

Launching a Dream

For fourteen years, Sam Shelton, principal with Jeff Fabian at KINETIK Communication Graphics in Washington, D.C., dreamed of launching a gallery where graphic design would be exhibited. As with many worthwhile ventures, encouragement from peers and friends was plentiful. It was the practicalities—time and money—that held him back.

Would his dream bleed him or his existing business dry? Would he have enough energy to get the gallery off the ground? Shelton says that his success so far—the gallery has been open since June 2000—is a result of careful planning and of not knowing what in the world would be next.

The same thing that drove Sam Shelton to start KINETIK Graphic Communications with partner Jeff Fabian in 1988 compelled him to found Kitchen [K], A Design Gallery, in Washington, D.C.: a dream that turned into a passion that grew into a reality.

A dream is passive, he says. But a passion is assertive and forces you to do something, anything. "It's the passion that feeds the idea and keeps it alive," Shelton says. "It keeps the idea on the right track."

The gallery, which is housed in the same building as the KINETIK offices, has hosted travelling and one-time shows by the AIGA and other design-related organizations. Partners Shelton, Fabian, and

Beverly Hunter keep the gallery and the design business separate so that people don't misconstrue it as a marketing effort. Their sole purpose is to educate the public about design.

Harnessing the Passion

Everyone has dreams of one sort or another. But the passion necessary to ignite a dream is a bit like electricity: It can be very effective if it can be channeled properly—easier said than done, explains Shelton. Start by getting a handle on one's own passion, he advises.

"I have found that it takes me a while to go through many revisions of my plan in my brain before I am ready to talk about it with other people," Shelton says. "You have to put the plan into writing. It's the same advice you hear all of the time: Have a business plan. Be able to articulate what that plan is in a way that will harness other people's passion."

With his business and the gallery, Shelton has found himself in a position not unlike a plane taxiing down a runway. "I can't take off. There is not enough of my own passion to get the plane off the ground. I need other people's passion before we can fly."

Often, getting the support of peers isn't as tough as inspiring the enthusiasm of the outside professionals one needs to handle the realities of a new venture: lawyers, accountants, bankers, and insurance people. They are much more apt to cast a baleful eye on any developing idea. But rather than regarding their advice as a cold, wet blanket, Shelton is re-energized.

"It helps so much to talk with them. They question us and force us to dig deeper, to figure out things we don't want to face. They also ask questions, in the case of the gallery, about areas we were not familiar with—the gallery world, the non-profit world, about having visitors actually coming into our space, and so on," he says.

Harnessing the Energy

In the beginning, Shelton, Fabian, and Hunter believed that running the gallery would be akin to handling a project from a client. When it was time to organize a show, they would come up with a plan to present (to themselves), do the design, and so forth. In reality, however, they discovered that they were hard clients. Clients provide feedback in terms of a "yes" or a "no," and they offer suggestions for improvement.

If a client made an ill-advised decision, that was their responsibility. But stepping into the role of client meant that the designers would have to bear the full brunt of whatever happened: They found themselves full of second-guesses and indecisiveness.

To combat this drain on their energies, they separated the staff into two teams: one that tackled the design problem and the other that acted as the "client," offering criticism and advice. Ultimately, it was this second group that gave the first group the green light to proceed.

But anyone launching a new venture must be prepared to handle wrong turns when they do occur. For instance, before the gallery opened, Shelton and his partners drew up a cash flow plan based on membership and grant revenue. With a recession and other world events in late 2001 and early 2002, these projections have turned out to be unrealistic. As much as they don't like it, KINETIK is still supporting the gallery to a great extent.

In addition to managing money, time must be guarded carefully. "One of the best lessons I have learned is that I have to set limits for myself and decide what is going to be done, when," Shelton says. Otherwise, the demands of his business and the gallery would fill every waking moment. "I had to be willing to delegate and let some things go. I had to become able to accept the results of other people's actions."

For a designer used to controlling minute levels of detail, this can be tough. But with a second venture in motion, things happen quickly, he says. Letting others help manage your dream is crucial.

At the same time, it's just as important to be aware of the time your new flight plan takes away from others, whether it is a family at home, a business partner, or employees. It's unrealistic to ask others to embrace the same personal sacrifices you are making, Shelton says.

Handling Reality

Perversely, one concept that Shelton and his partners have kept in sight since the start of Kitchen [K] is that of failure. The reality, the designer says, is that most new endeavors do fail. But even at their lowest point in KINETIK's beginnings, Shelton and Fabian felt they were learning valuable lessons, lessons that today are helping them cope with Kitchen [K]. Hard times can be the best teacher, if one is willing to pay attention.

"We barely had enough money to pay the rent and got groceries from my parents. That was the only way we survived," he recalls. It was a time to learn about developing a diversified client base, the value of credit from a banking partner, the benefit of realistic cash reserves, and other lessons.

Another, more pleasant reality, is that of charting one's own course. Shelton feels that both KINETIK and Kitchen [K] are achieving their respective goals now, and he gets great satisfaction from watching them fly. Another payoff is hosting yet another environment where he can nurture people and guide them toward their dreams.

Finally, Shelton admits that naïveté may have been one of his greatest allies in the creation of Kitchen [K]. "We could have spent years learning everything we should have known. But the reality is that we went by the seat of our pants; we learned as we went along. If we had waited to learn what we didn't know, we never would have done it—it would have been much too scary."

There has to be a plan. There has to be professional help for financial and legal matters, he says. But you don't have to know all of the answers when you start something new.

"You won't know all of the questions either," he adds.

The week Shelton was interviewed for this article, he was in his first few days of a month-long sabbatical, arranged so that he could figure out what he wants to do next. He still loves his work and the gallery, but feels it's time for some self-reflection.

Dreams need attention, he knows. Unless their owners spend plenty of time with them, can properly visualize where they might go, and then begin to ignite the imagination of others with their possibilities, they remain just that: dreams with nowhere to go.

DESIGNKITCHEN

Sharpening Focus on Core Strengths

A lot of design offices talk about being brand consulting firms, but what they are really offering is exactly the same services they always have. It's a shame, since now more than ever, clients need a true integration between business and design in order to survive.

Designkitchen, Chicago, has made the commitment and kept it. In most people's minds, Designkitchen is still a traditional design firm. But once clients have a face-to-face meeting with the firm's principals, they can start to understand and appreciate the office's new direction.

"We think like business people, and though the work is artful, we have no illusions about art. Our work aims to support competitive advantage."

That short excerpt from Designkitchen's Web site, in a nutshell, defines how the ten-year-old, twenty-five-person firm is different from your typical design agency. Creative director and president Sam Landers and his team aim to run a high-octane mix of business and design. But their true point of differentiation is their ability to integrate on- and off-line strategies.

"'One brand message. Multiple platforms.' That has been our push for the last two-and-a-half years," explains Landers. Previously, the company could be described as a traditional design firm.

"It was less a way to differentiate our company from others, and more a recognition of what is happening around us. The acceleration of the Internet and access to information has created huge gaps in the traditional world of communications," he says. Companies with expertise in print, broadcast, and the Web were not partnering or consolidating—and all of those components needed to be brought together in order to improve the audience's communication experience. "I felt strongly that technology and the Web were going to become a point of entry for many of us in business—and as consumers—to learn about services and new products."

Landers says that Designkitchen has been in the brand consulting business for many years—before the "B" mantra became so pervasive. But with so many other design firms jumping on the bandwagon, the firm's solution was to add business and technology elements that most design firms didn't have, while keeping the design and branding arms that high tech firms couldn't offer. Additionally, they are partnering with companies who have strong IT capabilities, but who are not focused on site design and branding.

"A lot of print firms have tried to grow their capabilities," Landers says. "We don't have a lot of competition from design firms anymore. Three years ago, we were competing against huge technology and consulting companies, but they were not offering a branding component. Firms don't come to you just because they need a logo anymore: They also need a movie they can stream on-line, or a Web site, or whatever."

The Changeover

For Designkitchen, the fully integrated approach definitely was the way to go. After the new business plan was drawn up, Landers shared it with the staff. While the new ideas were exciting, he knew they could also cause anxieties and uncertainties. So keeping the plan clear and simple was crucial, as was maintaining the channels of communication so that there is a constant exchange of ideas.

"Staff members were cautious, as you would expect from a group of smart people," Landers recalls. The plans could not be forced on them: Instead, the staff needed to see the benefit for them. "It's important to understand that talented people like this want opportunities to do good work. Align their career goals with that of the business."

The staff embraced the new plans. Today, the Designkitchen staff is grouped in five clearly defined, primary teams: Business Assessment; Business/Creative Integration; Design; Interactive; and Client Management. Staff members understand their own roles and those of their coworkers more completely, and so they are better able to explain the company and its focus to clients.

"This more immediate view of what we are galvanizes us as a company. Now that we have close to forty people on two floors, we know—scheduling- and job-wise—what everybody is doing. Every Monday without fail we meet in our teams," Landers explains. The regular show-and-tell sessions constantly update everyone's view of the company.

Pre-flight Advice

For any firm owner who is planning to change the personality or scope of his or her business, Landers says the changeover can be slow to sink into clients' consciousness'. Outsiders know you as they have always known you, not as you want to be known. With all of the changes Designkitchen has made in the past few years, it has been tough getting the news out to everyone. Face-to-face meetings are best, but these take time. To help the process along, Landers is talking to a public relations firm to get the word out.

Also prior to any change in the old flight plan, take a good, hard look at your staff. Can they do what you envision, or is it time to bring in specialists? "We have had to hire employees who are really businesspeople," Landers says, "which still feels like something of an anomaly. One-third of our people are client and brand-strategy focused; they are not designers."

To help himself stay focused on the Designkitchen goals, Landers observes other agencies that have made the successful transition to a more heavily business-directed group. "VSA has done a great job of integrating business acumen with design. Pentagram is great, too: They do very artistic work, but when you see how they are addressing the client's business objectives, the design becomes transparent. You really get a sense of the brand of the client's company."

Landers says his firm's shift toward driving the branding and content management of Web and print projects together is what clients will be desiring very soon. His staff stands poised and ready, slightly ahead of the curve.

KBDA

Kim Baer has relatives in the real estate business. Why, they asked the principal of the design firm KBDA, do you continue to lease these awful spaces, spend plenty of time and money transforming them into livable but not ideal office space, and then have to move? Designers have a unique ability to transform things: Why not transform a space into something you love and own?

Why indeed, Baer asked herself. In 2001, she decided to take the plunge. She bought a building she describes as a mess, and she and her staff took on the eight-month renovation. It was a move that has recast the direction—and certainly the efficiency—of her office.

What's the best thing about KBDA's new space in West Los Angeles? Storage, says principal Kim Baer.

"It sounds silly. But the fact that there is a place for everything and workflow has been taken into account has made a huge difference. I realized how much time we were spending looking for things. All of the storage is behind closed doors now. It used to be time-consuming to prepare for clients coming to our old offices. Now we feel fine about having clients drop in," she says.

The old office had been the twenty-year-old design office's home for fifteen years. Rents were escalating, and Baer had had the unpleasant experience of being evicted by a greedy landlord before: She had no desire to go through that again. Over the years, she had spent thousands of dollars trying to shape unshapeable spaces, some in questionable neighborhoods, to better fit her firm's needs.

Another deciding factor: She herself felt ready to make a commitment. Prior to that, she needed the flexibility of being able to walk away from it all if she wished. It was time, she decided, to move into a space that was KBDA's.

"I had read enough about recruiting issues over the years to know that a good workspace is as important to designers as anything else," Baer reports. "We wanted a space that was not typical, something suited to our culture."

The two biggest things they wanted at the start of their search was an outdoor area and a kitchen. Food is a big part of the studio's culture: Many a celebration and everyday meetings are held with a meal as a centerpiece. An outdoor area would provide light and air, as well as space for the studio's dogs and Koi pond.

A Real Find

When Baer and her designers first laid eyes on the space they eventually purchased, it bore no resemblance to their wish list. It was dark and covered in paneling and shag carpeting. The ceilings were pock-marked with fluorescent lights. It was tough for even a talented group of designers to see its potential.

But the space had its advantages: It was in a safe neighborhood, and it cut at least fifteen minutes off of everyone's commute, a major employee perk in LA, where traffic is always a headache. It was close to restaurants and services that employees wanted. And since the space would have to be torn down to the studs, it could be crafted into just about anything they wanted. Baer bought the place.

In six months time, the budget and schedule had been doubled, but Baer and her staff are now comfortably ensconced in a skylit space with restored brickwork, full of cabinets, conference rooms, and common areas that were crafted especially for them.

Of course, the transformation was not without its headaches. Here's what the team learned:

- Carefully study your existing space and dream about how it could be better. Make specific lists of space planning needs and ask you contractor to help devise solutions. For example, place supplies for maximum efficiency. Set up areas for equipment you frequently use. Detailing it all out in advance will help you later.
- Don't be in a rush as you make big decisions. If you are, you will not be able to think things out completely, and cost and time spent continue to go up.

"Ironically, there is a parallel in our world, when we have clients who are in an enormous rush. We were making a lease payment and a mortgage at the time. The architect suggested we could save time by getting a construction bid based on rough plans," says Baer, adding that she would never do that again. "Sure, we may have gotten in here a month or two sooner, but we spent much more money on change orders than we would have on another month's lease."

The contractor had made his bid based on Baer's original plans, which changed as details and materials were finalized. "I am sure this is how our clients feel when they need to sign change orders. We should have taken the time to do a set of detailed plans," she notes.

- When you buy a space, be rational, not emotional. Your business's well-being is at stake.
- Designate an internal project manager as the main contact for the architect and contractor. You need someone on staff who is well-versed in construction or else buy a space that doesn't need quite so much work. At KBDA, one staff per-

son was hired to manage the process. "My job was to keep the business running," says Baer.

• Talk with other studios who have been through the process before: They have invaluable firsthand experience.

• Talk to your staff about what they want. In the company's old space, an open layout, sound was always an issue. Baer surveyed her employees on a number of issues before the move and was surprised at what a large concern it was: People liked to work in open areas because they liked to interact, but they couldn't concentrate.

So in the new space, there is a closed conference room. In addition, they spent extra money for carpeting and double-glazed windows to keep the ambient sound down.

• You can purchase a lousy space in a nice neighborhood for roughly the same money as you can get a nice office in an lousy neighborhood. The KBDA staff felt that they could fix the office but couldn't do much about the neighborhood, so they chose the former.

• Planning a new space requires enormous effort, so it makes sense to involve staff whenever possible. They will feel much more ownership in the new office, and the eventual move will not be nearly as traumatic.

In fact, Baer was a little worried about "homesickness" following the move. After all, she and her staff had been in the old space for a long time and had a certain amount of fondness for it, despite its shortfalls.

"In one day after moving, we had forgotten that we were ever there. It taught me that if you do it right, you won't ever think of your old space again," she says.

Everything Is New Again

What else has changed for KBDA? Financially, the firm has a lower monthly mortgage than its old lease, and the payments will never increase. It no longer has to worry about the vagaries of an unreasonable landlord. Their new space has been custom-fitted, so productivity has increased.

But perhaps most important is the pride Baer and her staff feel when they walk in the front door every day. It is a healthy environment, full of the aesthetic concerns designers respond to. They also have a space that appeals to clients. Baer finds that the new office permits clients to experience the company's design sensibilities in a very tangible way. As a marketing tool, the new space has been very effective: When clients walk in, they often say they would like to live there.

MELVÆR & LIEN

Presenting a Brand-New Face

In 1989, Melvær and Lien found itself to be a successful although stan-dard provider of annual reports, brochures, profiles, and so on—all the usual fodder of the business-to-business world. Its owners, Ståle Melvær and Andreas Lien, knew it was a safe business, but it was one that would soon be a threat to their employees' creativity. A threat to creativity would soon jeopardize the company's ability to make a profit.

So Melvær, Lien, and four new partners transformed the company, changing it from a typical design agency to what they now call an "idea entrepreneur" group. They believe it is a philosophy that not only inspires their staff, but which also dramatically assists clients in their business.

M&L was feeling quite uncomfortable about its feeling of balance in 1998. Business was steady. There was always a client at the end of all processes. The brief would be delivered, it would be addressed, and the product would be picked up. The company's partners called it a "slumber situation."

Was this type of balance healthy for their business? It certainly felt safe. Or, to find the real balance point, perhaps they needed to dis-turb the equilibrium. It was at that point the firm's partners, Ståle Melvær, Andreas Lien, Biarne Uldal, Bjørn Ragnar Bastiansen, Kjell Ramsdal, and Tone Michaelsen, came up with the idea of the "idea entrepreneur," an entirely new direction for the twenty-five-person firm, based in Stavanger, Norway.

"An idea entrepreneur is a company that transforms ideas into good business," explains partner Ståle Melvær. "How to handle the potential power of an idea is [our] core business. We try to find quality where there is, literally speaking, nothing."

The group has developed methods, tools, and techniques that help them catch the value of otherwise "empty" ideas. Ideas, Melvær says, are the building blocks. His company's entrepreneurship provides the implementation that actually builds something.

An example: In 2000, two individuals approached M&L with an idea: a unique method of analyzing and providing information about the carbon market. They wanted to call the company "Climdex," Melvær recalls.

After a hectic and fun two-month period, the company, renamed "Point Carbon," was ready to present itself to the world. Melvær&Lien had taken a good product that could be sold any number of ways and had defined it as a solid business product with a complete company profile, an effective Web site, and professionally designed marketing materials.

One year later, Point Carbon is regarded as the global leader in its niche and has an impressive customer list. The M&L system works, says Melvær.

A Change in Direction

Melvær felt that transforming his company from a design-only firm to a business incubator plus design firm was important for several reasons. First of all, he believed he could serve his clients better. People with good ideas, such as inventors, scientists, and entrepreneurs, have several options when trying to turn their idea into a successful business: They can go to a management consultancy and ask for assistance, or they could approach venture capitalists and ask for money. In any scenario, they must go to several different parties in order to gain all of the expertise needed to get their idea off the ground.

Both of these options, while they do solve some problems for the entrepreneur, neglect to address other major stumbling blocks.

"For instance, these suggested partners would not have the needed branding and marketing experience. Even worse for start-ups is that these are long-winded, tiring processes which would drain the new company of both ownership and resources," Melvær explains.

Rather than rely on this "relay approach" to starting a business, the entrepreneur can come to Melvær&Lien and have all of the assistance it needs from one source, even funding. From a more sharply defined business idea and new business name, to a brand identity, Web page and marketing materials, the new business would be completely outfitted in a short period of time.

The second reason Melvær transformed his company was to re-inspire his staff. The "safe" business that they had before the changeover certainly involved quality work, but he felt that his staff was stagnating. When stagnation occurs, the love and interest a designer had for the skill itself is vanishing.

"I truly believe that stagnation is a result of letting the surroundings take too much control of your work. Letting clients or colleagues [have too much] influence on choices that need to be made leaves the designer less passionate and less confident," Melvær says.

The new "idea entrepreneur" approach gave the designers the room they needed to use their creativity on any project they felt was worthy, whether there was a client involved or not. (At least three of the ideas M&L staffers have created have been turned into self-running companies.) When the staff is challenged, they are more satisfied. When they are more satisfied, they are more likely to stay with the firm, improving the principal's ROI on their training.

"The feeling of actually contributing to the creation of a product or business is much more attractive to staff than purely producing material for a huge client," Melvær explains.

Fear of Change

Of course, these changes were quite radical for the company. Melvær says the partners tried to minimize staff apprehension by inviting everyone into the transition process. Plenum meetings were held, and discussions bounced back and forth until some agreements could be reached. Melvær knows that the changes will probably be an ongoing process, though, and that his company will always be in change-mode.

The fear vanishes with knowledge and information, Melvær says. "We have no secrets in our organization, and we strongly believe that the problems we get from an extreme open-door policy is small compared to what a more traditional, from-the-top-down thinking would have given us."

To keep everyone up to date, the firm holds meetings and workshops often, and the partners make sure that everybody is challenged to speak out. Melvær acknowledges that his company's relatively small size facilitates direct communication, but it's the idea of not fearing open communication that is important.

The field of design will change dramatically in the next five to ten years, Melvær believes. Its merger with advertising will become even more pronounced. Pure design will no longer be enough, he says.

"There has to be more depth and intellectual drama to it. This design/drama combination will become a significant differentiator in the future," Melvær says.

In addition, crossover between other disciplines and design will occur more and more often. Be ready for opportunities, Melvær says: Breaking barriers can be very energizing for designers. Dare to learn about businesses far from your own. Talk to professionals in those fields—venture capitalists, private investors, researchers, educators—to gain their insights on design and communication.

The key to happiness, he says, is to always challenge your creativity. "Stop looking at yourself as a designer, and start thinking of yourself as a deliverer of ideas," he insists.

Part Six:

LEAVING

Section 14: It's My Party and I'll Fly If I Want To

Leaving One Firm and Starting Another

What designer doesn't dream of walking away from it all to start over in his or her own office? Even current design firm owners will admit that the idea has its attractions. But being fed up is one of the worst possible reasons to set out on your own.

Here, four different designers tell how and why they considered leaving—and in three cases, they did leave— very established positions to strike out on their own. The lessons they have learned are hard-won, and not everything has been rosy. But they're not looking back.

MITRE DESIGN

A Firm Splits in Two

Those who are familiar with the gorgeous, emotional work Henderson Tyner Art Company produced for clients such as American Express, Coca-Cola, Nabisco, Strathmore Paper, and IBM were definitely sad when they learned that its founders, Hayes Henderson and Troy Tyner, had decided to dissolve their partnership and open up their own offices.

Even good things have to come to an end, they say, and both are looking forward to even better days and work ahead. In this article, Tyner shares what he learned from the breakup and how he has gotten his new firm off to a solid start.

Deciding to part ways with friend and partner Hayes Henderson was not an easy conclusion for Troy Tyner. For eight years, the duo had run a very successful design/illustration hybrid agency in Winston-Salem, North Carolina, accommodating large, deep-pocketed clients as well as small clients with no pockets at all. Along the way, they picked up their share of awards, including recognition from The New York Art Director's Club, the AIGA, Type Director's Club, The 100 Show, and nearly every design publication.

But the partners' visions for the company had begun to change. The dynamics of a growing staff and changing business climate at Henderson Tyner was compounding their differences of opinion: Staying on the same page or even having time to really discuss it was becoming very difficult. Tyner saw an opportunity to create a new design firm that would keep the office environment and the work intimate.

Tyner says that splitting with a partner is something that no one is every ready for: You could never plan for it enough. "The idea can be looming around for the longest time, but it is just not recognized or easily addressed. As soon as the concept of parting ways is mentioned, it becomes real and can happen quickly. Until then, you are swept up in your work and commitments: You just lose touch with what it is you really want to do," Tyner says.

Today, Tyner is operating Mitre Design out of a unique studio crafted from an old firehouse in Winston-Salem. Two senior members of his original staff members came with him, and he has since added new talent to the mix.

Handling the Split

The primary issues to keep in mind when considering a split in partnership are your personal goals. Ideally, at the start of the partnership, personal and company goals are usually closely matched. But, says Tyner, as time goes by and practical business concerns insert their spiny heads, one's own aspirations can be shunted to the side.

Tyner finally had to face what was making him unhappy. "I wanted to do the kind of work that having a larger company did not allow you to do, such as work with small to mid-size clients or individuals with a limited budget," he says. "Having business partners or a larger company to feed can sometimes dictate the criteria for accepting work. Staying lean gives you the flexibility to diversify. Now, we're just big enough to get the work done, but small enough to enjoy the process. Our size allows us to truly collaborate with our clients and each other, making the success of a project even more rewarding."

The ability to achieve balance is where the new company's name came from. "A mitre is the joining of opposing sides to create stability.

It's a synthesis—strategic and intuitive. It's doing work that is good business and work that is good will, finding the middle ground between working and living."

Being fully prepared to set out on his own again was a challenge, and it was not without its share of nerves. But it is much like how it was eight years ago, when he was gainfully employed as a senior art director at a successful agency, had just bought a new house, and he and his wife were expecting twins.

"I guess some people would say starting a business under those circumstances was not very wise. But if you don't overthink it, it's much easier to get things done," he laughs. "You have to say, 'How am I going to get this done?', not 'I wonder if this is going to fail.'"

Tyner did not leave Henderson Tyner empty-handed. The company had always operated like two agencies: Both principals had their own accounts and pet projects. Staff split almost naturally between the two tracks. Since there was little collaboration between the two groups, it was easy to divide accounts.

Preparing to leave was difficult. Of course, Tyner and Henderson both wanted to continue working with existing clients after the split, but in cultivating these relationships, had to be careful not to stray into each other's territory. It might have helped to have had some sort of agreement on paper that spelled out exactly what would happen if the agency dissolved, Tyner says. That being said, he knows that no document could cover every eventuality.

"There is no fail-safe arrangement. When starting a company, certain preparations should be made in the event a split occurs down the road, but even these will just be a place to start discussions if that time ever comes," Tyner says. "But you don't step into a business partnership all the while you are preparing an exit strategy, or you will never give it a chance to succeed. It's a leap of faith."

Repeat Performances

Would he go into partnership again? Yes, he says, but under different circumstances. He learned a great deal about himself, business, and human dynamics in his eight-year partnership.

"It was the right thing to do when we started, but it seems miles away from where I am now," he says.

It is so important to take precautions regardless of how good your relationship is with the other person, he says. Business issues will creep into the personal relationship, but they do not have to poison it.

"Approach the partnership in the same way you would if you were going into business with a stranger. Formalize your partnership, get legal advice, get personal advice, and be objective," Tyner adds.

Every situation is unique. Some partnerships thrive, while others fail quickly. So Tyner's advice is simple.

"For anyone considering getting in or out of a partnership: Be honest with yourself. Keep a constant check on what will make you happy, and be willing to make the changes needed to get there. The risks will never outweigh the rewards or the satisfaction of having something that is yours."

EROWE DESIGN

A Fledgling Firm Owner Reflects

At one time or another, every designer/employee dreams of it: Setting out on one's own to open his or her own office. Sure, there will be headaches. Yes, they understand that money and their guts will be tight most of the time. But every year, hundreds of designers strike out on their own.

The sad news is that most of these businesses will fail. The reasons why are obvious: No business plan, not enough funding, no need for that business's services or products. Adam Rowe of erowe design, San Diego, is determined to beat the odds with a bit of luck, common sense, and the ability to stay calm.

When Adam Rowe decided to turn his freelance business, erowe design, into his full-time employment, the timing could not have been more curious. He was employed as a senior art director at Qualcomm, at that time a market darling with soaring stock values. His portfolio worth was growing daily; in fact, he would call the e-trade hotline almost every morning just to have the pleasure of hearing the pre-recorded woman's voice tell him his net worth.

But he was also thinking about opening his own full-time shop. As time passed and he continued to consider, the economy soured. By the time he was really ready to open his doors in late 2001, recession had drifted over the landscape.

"Some people thought I was crazy given the timing," recalls Rowe, who had actually left full-time positions several times before with the full intent of setting out on his own, only to be offered another position elsewhere. "But a dear friend of mine who has had her own studio for ten years and who also opened up in the depths of recession asked me, 'What better time is there to enter the marketplace? There is no where to go but up.'

"It was time to get this bird off the ground rather than fall back into the safety net of working for someone else and the security of a steady paycheck," he adds.

Eliminate Debt

Rowe wanted to start his business debt-free. It's impossible, he says, to try to pay off debt and get new work at the same time. He established a fund that contained some of the value of his Qualcomm stock that would not only help him set up his new office, but which also enabled him to make house and car payments for a year. For Rowe, having this financial comfort zone was necessary from a psychological standpoint. He knows he was extremely lucky in this regard.

"Just having that cushion added value to this business. Before you leave your current employer, you have to be in a position where you can take from 15 to 25 percent of your paycheck and save it for equipment or insurance or whatever. Everything is expensive when you are on your own. You can look at your own home phone bill, for example, and triple it to understand what the cost will be to bring lines into the new office," he says.

The Business Plan

Rowe says having a business plan is a good idea for any designer because, for the most part, designers have not gone to business school and are not well-versed on such matters. He worked with his financial advisor to verbalize and record where he wanted to take his studio.

Even in his first year, the direction he has taken is vastly different from the plan he had originally recorded: Projects that he never anticipated have been dropped into his lap. Deviating from the plan is not a problem, he says, as long as the overall goals are kept in view.

He has discovered that although his original plan did not include a business development person, he has now hired a freelance professional to do that work. He was naïve, Rowe says, to think he would be able to follow up on referrals and client inquiries, self-promotions, and still do design all in the same work day.

Another part of the business plan should include whether or not one wants employees. Rowe has discovered that, from a paperwork standpoint, having one employee is as much work as having 100. Also, having employees means that the machine gets bigger and its appetite increases exponentially. Rowe has chosen to maintain a virtual office where he has space and facilities for about five designers, account people, and architects to work as subcontractors.

"I knew of one person who landed a multi-million dollar assignment. He ended up hiring eight or nine people to finish the job, and became so involved with this one client that when the project was over, he had to let all of the employees go and had to eventually start his business over gain," Rowe says. "No client should be any more than 15 to 25 percent of any small business's clientele, and I think that 25 percent is really pushing it."

Support Structure

Rowe feels lucky to be working in San Diego, a city where most designers and vendors have known each other for years and where people tend to look out for you. But he also believes that getting support from others means giving back. Be an active member of the local AIGA, he says; professional organizations are a self-perpetuating cycle of support.

Rowe also reaches out into the community for support from professionals with other areas of expertise: architects, new media people, technical support people, and more. There is almost no way to be a one-man shop today and do everything well. Collaborating with other professionals constantly breathes fresh air into his work, and he thinks the reverse is probably true as well.

Finally, Rowe consciously seeks support from clients. He makes sure he selects clients who value what he does, clients who share his enthusiasm are the best allies a designer can have.

"I think the client relationship is such a huge part of any individual studio's success. Without their encouragement and belief in your building an ongoing dialogue, one cannot succeed. My clients are my friends and confidants: We're looking out for each other well beyond the project work."

Staying Calm

The scariest thing about being out on one's own, as any designer knows, is that you are only as good as your last job.

"I'm always wondering if the phone is ever going to ring again," Rowe says.

But it is extremely important to remain calm and focused on the big picture. Everyone needs challenge on a daily basis, he says: This is stress, but it is the good kind of stress, the kind that keeps him moving.

Another factor that can be somewhat disorienting to new design firm owners is having to step into many different roles. Where before a person might have been a designer, suddenly he or she is everything to everybody.

"The strangest thing about doing this is that some days I am the accountant, sometimes I am the father, and some days I am a diplomat," he notes. You can't be a "type B" person, hanging back and waiting for others to take action. When your internal clock tells you it's time to strike out on your own, you have to be ready to step into any role: Designing will not be your full-time job anymore.

ART CHANTRY

On Leaving One's Stomping Grounds

When Art Chantry left Seattle for St. Louis, he in some ways left part of himself behind. The artist and designer is credited by many for having defined the design atmosphere for the entire Northwest for many years. But in the end, business concerns drove him east.

Today, he is sorry he had to leave, but happy in his new locale, and he is already sweeping regional design competitions with his work. The lessons he learned in leaving were hard-won: Chantry wishes he could have stayed put, but reality insisted otherwise.

Art Chantry is always saying things that clients and peers don't like to hear. Let the business eat you alive: It's the only way to get the best work. Designers seek constant love and approval on a daily basis. Graphic design has more to do with babysitting and tricking people than it has to do with making pictures.

There is no way you can be in this business, he says, without going into a lot of dark spaces and saying things that make people uncomfortable. Many designers would agree with what he believes, but they wouldn't say so out loud. That's what got him in trouble and eventually at least in part forced him out of his beloved hometown.

"I left town for very personal reasons," Chantry says. "I developed a style that became a regional style, but I couldn't survive there with it. I was treated as an outsider because of what I believed. Everyone—ex-employees, competitors, whomever—competed with me for what was really a very small portion of the market."

He moved his studio twelve times in fifteen years as rents sky-rocketed. Every time he moved, his income dropped, to the point where he earned about $4,000 in the year 2000.

"I was prolific as hell, and I really had to crank. Eventually, I was burned out because I had to work so hard all the time," he recalls. Friends who have stayed in the Seattle area—and there aren't many left—found the same thing. Monster agencies would swoop in and take even their smallest clients away, even freebie accounts.

The Move

His girlfriend was enduring the same experience: She is a great designer, Chantry says, but couldn't find a job that paid well enough. So she got in touch with a headhunter, who in relatively short order asked if she was willing to relocate: There were plenty of great jobs elsewhere. She decided on St. Louis. Chantry decided to follow.

"I am very bitter about leaving Seattle—it's my home," he says. "I love it there. Unfortunately, so did everyone else."

Moving was expensive, financially and personally. Expect to leave your entire life behind. The older one is, the larger the circle of friends and business contacts you have, and the bigger the sacrifice it is to leave it behind. It really pays, Chantry says, to scout out the new area before you arrive and have at least one client lined up that you can use as a base on which to build.

Still, now that he has made the move to a completely new region, he finds that much of his work is still from the Northwest. He doesn't expect that to last, however. If you leave your client base behind, he says, don't necessarily expect it to follow you.

Illustrators and other artists who produce a product have an easier time working outside of their own geographic region, Chantry believes. But designers need human-to-human contact. That's why you don't see many designers reps, he adds: You really need to be there with the client.

"The psychology of it all is so intense, you need to be with the client to read his body language and expressions. Working from a distance only works if you are hyper-famous already, and even those designers find themselves on airplanes all the time," he notes.

Starting Over

Response to his work in St. Louis has been mixed. There is no other designer or artist quite like him there, and those who know him expect him to be doing punk rock stuff. Chantry says he may have to chuck that type of work altogether in order to build a new reputation, one that will land him jobs that pay better than punk rock bands or their labels do.

At the time of this writing, Chantry had a show of his work at the City Museum. So he has been received well. But jobs have yet to begin rolling in. He still feels he has found a gold mine in the Midwest, what with so many Fortune 500 companies located there and the cost of living so low.

He knows that many, especially young designers, flock to New York or Washington or San Francisco to work because they seem so fashionable and prestigious. But unless you are very young or very rich, Chantry advises against such moves. These are cities full of elitism and nightmares, he believes. People come to those cities to work, stay for about two years, and then head off to find a better quality of life.

"You may need to dispose of your ideas of being hip [working in the Midwest], but you can do quality work for quality clients in an area like this," Chantry says.

The artist was also pleasantly surprised at how authentically nice people are in his new hometown—a perk in itself, especially after the drubbing he has already taken.

As far as finding more local work is concerned, Chantry says he is starting from scratch. Nobody there knows about his history or achievements, nor do they seem to care.

He is investigating three fronts to increase workload: First, he is talking with a rep who concentrates on "stylized" designers like himself. Second, he and his girlfriend are working on self-developed projects (books, mostly) which have attracted the attention of several publishers.

Third, he is beginning to sell samples of his work on e-bay. "It sounds silly, but it turns my approach from a service orientation to a product orientation," Chantry explains. "I don't need to rely so heavily on clients."

There is a fourth possibility, he says.

"I've been approached by four colleges and universities out here about teaching, but they stopped returning my phone calls once they met me. I really don't come off as very 'academic,'" he notes. "Go figger."

BO BOTHE/SAVAGE DESIGN GROUP

On Not Leaving

Like many employed designers, Bo Bothe sometimes dreamed about leaving his current situation and opening up his own studio. He would make the decisions; he would select the clients to target. He would have real control over his own show.

And then, without ever quitting his job, he got just that opportunity: His employer, Paula Savage of Savage Design Group, Houston, Texas, offered him partnership in her firm. He would have more ability to help determine the future direction of the company and certainly more responsibility, but with less of the risk normally associated with opening a new office. Here, the design director talks about his decision.

In this book's chapter on leaving, it seems fitting to end with a story about not leaving—in other words, deciding to stay. Bo Bothe, design director at Savage Design Group, stayed because his boss, Paula Savage, made him an offer that made leaving seem like a decidedly unwise option: She offered him partnership in her successful company.

In accepting, he became the seventh partner at Savage Design (including Paula), a twenty-five-person firm that specializes in corporate communications design. One individual has been a partner with the firm for fifteen years; Bothe and three others are the most recent partners. Savage got agreement from her other two partners, Kenny Ragland and Dahlia Salazar, prior to offering partnership to Bothe and the other three individuals, but ultimately, it was her decision as majority owner.

He had thought about leaving Savage Design Group before to open his own office, not because he was unhappy, but because he has always had an entrepreneurial streak. But with two children at home, he was very rooted, and the partnership offered a kind of security he hadn't anticipated. There is a real comfort in knowing that there is a group of very talented designers and communicators working on behalf of his welfare, he says.

So in terms of keeping senior staff on board, Bothe feels that Savage's strategy is a good one, although to the outsider, buying in to a firm might appear to be a rather backward arrangement. But the design director feels he is getting real value with his purchase.

"It seems like an odd way to hold on to people, offering someone equity at a cost. But I don't have to struggle to build a new client base, as I would in my own office. These are tough times. Paula has a great reputation; aside from the talent and infrastructure, that's really what we buy into," he explains. Bothe took out a loan to finance his purchase of company stock, even though Savage offers to finance potential partners. In five years, the total value of stock will be paid out. At that point, Savage will still be the majority stockholder, and if she chose to leave the company, the remaining partners would have the opportunity to buy her out.

They do not know who would turn out to be the managing partner at that point. It's like they are all in training right now, each trying on the management role to see if it's a good fit. In the event that a partner would like to leave the company, the company will purchase back his or her shares. The agreement does not allow an outside person, especially a competitor, to still be a stakeholder.

Partnership Pluses

Bothe says that he was helping to direct the kind of business that Savage Design did even before he was a partner. Paula Savage is a very transparent sort of manager, so he could see how the business was being run and take part. Now that he is a partner, he feels that he is privy to the office's bigger picture, and that he has a say-so in setting its goals. Each of the seven partners—whether they are designers, art directors or marketing people—now have an understanding of the same goals.

The partners—each holds a different percentage of stock in the company—are free to voice their opinions, although Paula Savage, as majority owner, still has the final word in any decision. Nevertheless, Bothe feels that she is a very good listener.

"It would be easy for the majority business owner to go into her shell and say, 'This is how I handle this.' But the other partners here have different ideas, which she does consider. It's a neat collaboration," he believes.

Another plus: Growing the company now means growing his own investment. It's the next best thing to working for himself.

Recently, the partners held its yearly owners' retreat off site and talked frankly about where each of them wanted the company to go. Planning is essential to the group, because if Savage would decide to retire, there will be six strong-willed partners left to settle things. A plan that will be drafted before such a tumultuous change takes place is being discussed now, Bothe says.

Partnership Bound?

Everything must be out in the open, Bothe says, for a designer to consider going into a partnership. All books and folders should be opened.

"Your partners will become like family—and families do not always get along. But you and your partners should be able to compromise and work things out. Most of the time we agree to disagree," he says.

Section 15: To Boldly Go Where No Firm Has Gone Before

Breaking Into New Areas of Business

Graphic designers are prolific dreamers: They can imagine how their talents can be applied to any number of new projects or services. The trick, however, is changing the dream into a reality that doesn't sap the designer or his or her business of cash and energy. And although books on the subject of entrepreneurship abound, nobody has done exactly what you want to try. So there's no road map.

The following stories should offer guidance. Each is a real-world example of dreams coming true—as well as what to do when the dream turns out to be a nightmare. In the cold light of day, certain aspects of a plan might not look quite as dreamy as they did the night before.

HORNALL ANDERSON DESIGN WORKS

Changing In-House Culture

When it comes to new media, Hornall Anderson was a late-comer to the fray. Many competitors had gone out on the limb before them in a "me-too" frame of mind. But principal Jack Anderson says his firm waited until it could make a long-term commitment. In essence, they treated it as a new business within their existing business.

The new discipline had to be completely integrated with the existing company, though, not cobbled on like an afterthought. Anderson explains his company's tack into a brand-new area and why it took this particular route.

When entering a new area of business, says Jack Anderson of Hornall Anderson Design Works, Seattle, it can't be treated like an experiment or it doesn't come off like the real deal. If his firm hadn't treated its foray into new media seriously, it would have "come off as 'media design lite,'" he says.

Think of the new line of business like one of the three legs of a stool that you would be in trouble without, he says. It has to become a core competency of the company. "I can't imagine us without new media now. We think about all of the normal brand elements, but also the experience of new media."

Today, Hornall Anderson has some clients that only think of them as a new media firm. It's also a wonderful added value to offer to existing clients, the principal says—but you have to get out there and wave the flag over this great new offering that you have sunk money, time, and people into or else it won't take off.

He compares it to his firm's experience with environmental graphics: It has always been an added value for the company, not a core competency. It has great value, "but because we have never raised our flag high enough over it, we can get passed over on these jobs."

But with new media, Hornall Anderson jumped in feet-first. First, it hired twenty-five new employees and invested hundreds of thousands of dollars in new equipment to outfit them. It promoted its new offering; it got the word out to potential and existing clients through specialty mailings and presentations.

New media by Hornall Anderson was a hit outside of the office. But behind the company's doors, things were a bit different.

A Cultural Fit

New media and the changes it brought to the company, however, were initially a poor cultural fit for the company, Anderson explains.

"The company grew organically over fifteen years, and very slowly, we added people. When we jumped into new media—boom—twenty-five people were air-lifted into the organization over a one-and-a-half year period. They did not come in as interns, and they didn't earn their stripes in our fraternity or sorority. This was the age of the dot.com—bring your dog to work and play foosball. Their values were very different from ours, and their pay expectations were very different from what we were offering."

So began a rub of "we" and "they." Ultimately, all of the differences were smoothed out by integrating the new department throughout the company—everyone was mixed together across three floors. The principals made sure that projects were more completely integrated between traditional and new media.

Make certain, adds Anderson, that whatever ancillary area you add, that it is a good cultural as well as business fit.

Side Business or Smart Business?

How can a design firm owner know if what he or she wants to move into is a savvy business move or just something that might prove interesting? Graphic designers often pull from their heart-felt interests to create appendage businesses, very few of which ever earn any money, Anderson says.

"The fun in these is that you get to scratch an itch you couldn't before—it can be a tremendous creative outlet," he adds. But if it takes your eye off of the core competency of your original business, it will probably never be anything more than "something fun."

"There are only so many hours in the day," Anderson points out. "So much of the struggle in design firms today is with people who have their fingers in too many pies. They are spread too thin."

Diluting your own brand by trying to be all things to all people is another common error that design firms make. Not only are you sapping your mental and financial energies, it confuses clients. They want to know what your core competency is, not be amazed by a lengthy list of services.

If Starbucks decided to start selling car batteries, even though it is wildly famous for selling coffee, customers would stop thinking about the stores as cozy places to go relax, he points out. Pentagram is Anderson's "hero firm" in this regard: It consistently holds the line.

"When everyone else is getting fancy, they say, 'We do great design,'" he says.

Cutting Your Losses

Whenever a business owner is considering moving into a new area of business, that decision should never mortgage the original business financially or emotionally: That puts up a big yellow flag in front of clients and your employees.

Instead of putting everything at risk, use extra profits or a modest amount of equity to fund the new venture—and be prepared to lose that money. To give your efforts a fair chance, give the venture twelve months' worth of budget and attention, Anderson advises. "In about one year, you will know if this thing is making sense. But it really takes five years to prove that you have created a sustainable business," he adds. After the initial trial year, be prepared for no profit for the next three-and-a-half to four years.

Anderson notes that success in a new venture should not necessarily be defined as pulling a profit. Success might be breaking even, or it might be making a 20 percent margin. It's extremely difficult to define exactly what the "win" will be to yourself and with any partners ahead of time.

The Third Leg

New media has been a success for Hornall Anderson because *(a)* the firm chose not to be dabblers like so many other design firms, and *(b)* it easily could become that third leg of the stool that the company could not do without. It was not taken on because everyone else was doing it. Instead, Hornall Anderson incorporated the user interface element of new media to flush out all the components of a client experience it was already providing. Now, clients can see the true value in a full, integrated approach to solving their problems.

Extremely careful forethought and steering are what turns an adjunct into a core competency, Anderson says.

"There might be a designer who is thinking that it might be kind of fun to go into greeting cards—it could be a good sideline for his business and an outlet for his creativity. The next thing he knows, he has committed to a printer to print the things, he has no distribution, and a quarter of a million dollars invested in something he dreamed about over beers. He didn't think about having to go to the gift shows and about where the next half-million is going to come from to really get this show on the road," he says.

"At that point, it's too late to start fumbling around," Anderson adds.

LOGOLOUNGE, INC./GARDNER DESIGN

How to Start a Second Business

A waking dream can be as difficult to explain to other people as a dream one experiences while sleeping. It may feel very real to you, but trying to convince others to believe in it takes time.

Bill Gardner had a dream, a dream about a Web site that would replace the stacks and stacks of sticky-noted annuals and sourcebooks that he used in his identity and logo work. He stepped outside of the comfort zone of his successful graphic design firm, Gardner Design, of Wichita, Kansas, and left his fears of failure behind.

Back in 1994, an old friend of designer Bill Gardner's got back in touch with him. Recently divorced, the friend was at loose ends, with no idea of how to get back into the dating scene.

As the two friends discussed his difficulties, the subject of the Internet—then, very new to most laypeople—came up. Wouldn't it be great, mused the friend, not realizing how prophetic he was being, if you could meet people with common interests on the Internet?

Gardner mused out loud that someone interested in identity design like he is could have a site where people could share their logo designs.

The idea held a lot of appeal to Gardner, and it stuck with him. As a designer, he knew that design firms wanted to get exposure, and he definitely wanted to stay up-to-date with what was going on in his field. But he also believed that designers, including himself, spent entirely

too much money on buying books and entering competitions, particularly today, when every magazine and design organization hosts its own
fee-bearing events. The cachet of "winning" was being watered down.

"We have all done it for so long that none of us even think about
it anymore—it's just one of the costs of promoting yourself," he says. A
Web site could be an entirely new model: It would be searchable, easy
to update, and certainly more compact than a library full of publications
bristling with sticky notes.

But the dot.coms hadn't really happened yet, so there was no one
to go to with his questions. When he tried to explain this vision to other
people, he usually just stumped them.

Defining the Project

So Gardner continued to think about the project, often in the car while
travelling to Kansas City or St. Louis from Wichita and back again. The
site could help people promote themselves, he reasoned. In exchange,
he could charge for access to specialized information on the site. Key
designers could be invited to help launch the site. Once key designers
were on board to help launch the site, they would help attract lesser
known but talented designers.

The Web site would eventually become a community: He pictured
it as the ultimate go-to place for identity and logo designers.

Soon, technology caught up with his idea, and LogoLounge, Inc.,
was born. A membership-only destination, the site opened in the fall of
2001—unfortunately, with the worst timing possible. September's
tragedies had sapped everyone's energy, but the site had already con-
tracted to develop an annual of the best of work from its members.
Under less than ideal conditions, the project necessarily had to make a
slow and respectful launch.

In early 2002, less than six months old, the project had developed
a following of some of the world's most celebrated designers. To

launch the project, it had to be funded by Gardner's personal savings and by non-billable hours of his staff. He had put in countless hours of (thus far) unrecoverable time himself. Occasional technology headaches still had to be worked through, and membership was still is months away from where it needed to be.

So why would anyone who has a successful business already risk everything for an idea that may fail, as most new ventures do, at great personal and professional loss?

"For everything that has a downside, there is an equal and opposite upside," Gardner says. "I think many new business owners fail when they take on a venture alien to their previous experience. I tried to limit this project to something that I knew very well."

Gardner has limited his liability: LogoLounge is in debt to no one and makes no plans to take on debt beyond its resources. Too many projects are funded on monies the owners believe will come in. When it doesn't come, he says, the owners are caught by surprise.

Selling the Dream

But how do you get other people to buy into your dream? Because he has funded the project himself, there are no equity investors to satisfy. His employees at Gardner Design have actually been his biggest investors, in terms of their time and advice. They are the ones confronted with the extra work, during a time that is already economically challenging.

Gardner feels certain that an especially sensitive point is the amount of time that LogoLounge has required: It takes him away from his studio's tight-knit group. Now it's his duty to show employees that his reasons for starting LogoLounge will ultimately benefit all of them.

"Right now, it probably looks like a busman's holiday," he acknowledges. "But the larger picture is that this is not being done just to benefit me: We are creating added value together."

Entrepreneurial Advice

In addition to getting the support of those around you, Gardner says it is very important not to bite off more than you can chew. Financially, the new venture can't be the ruination of other ongoing projects. From a skill-set standpoint, recognize that you are going to need help. Gardner has brought in a programmer, a writer, and, most recently, a publicist. These people, too, have been brought in with the hope of future, not current, return.

Gardner had the advantage of having years to think through this project while he waited for technology to catch up with him. It gave him more time than most would have to think through every nuance of the process. Had he been forced to act at the time the concept was first envisioned, he knows his idea would have suffered.

"I would have lacked the ability to foster relationships with my partners as well as the ability to gain their insights and advice," Gardner says. Still, he doesn't have everything figured out. "Despite thinking I knew LogoLounge inside and out, my partners continue to surprise me with unexpected twists that had never occurred to me."

Finally, people often ask Gardner if running his own business—and now starting a second one—is scary. Of course, he replies. But he lessens his risk by surrounding himself with talented people and being able to roll with the changes.

"Lack of flexibility is the number one disease that kills most projects. That's not to say that you can't be committed to something," Gardner says. "You have a core idea, say of making white T-shirts. But if the people would rather have black T-shirts, you have to be flexible enough to make the change. After all, you are still making T-shirts."

Gardner is very satisfied with the growth of his idea. At this writing, LogoLounge, Inc. contains more than 7,000 logos from designers worldwide, and an annual containing 2,000 marks and feature articles on many world-class contributors has just been put to bed. The real-time, searchable aspects of the site will cause it to increase in value as more and more designers discover it. Gardner says it is a real pleasure to think of how much the site will have grown in another year or two. It's a pretty comforting feeling of acceptance, he says.

UNO HISPANIC ADVERTISING + DESIGN

The Benefits of a Very Defined Niche

"Thank you for calling UNO Hispanic Advertising: Branding for the new majority." That's the phone message that greets callers when they dial up Luis Fitch, founder of UNO Hispanic Advertising + Design. Fitch left the larger, corporate world of design to open his own small office and niche, that of design for the Hispanic market in North America.

His small company—just Fitch, his wife/partner Carolina, three designers, and an administrator—has landed some enormous clients, Target, Musicland, MTV Latino, and Mervyn's among them. They found themselves at the front edge of a now-evident trend, that the Hispanic population will eventually be the majority population in the United States.

When Luis Fitch was attending Art Center College, he asked the dean, James Miho, what is it that a designer should be doing today? Go back to your roots, the dean said. Be connected with your culture, whatever it is.

This turned out to be prophetic advice. Fitch, who ended up creating a very ethnic portfolio in college, has gone on to found a firm that is entirely centered on his heritage as a person of Mexican birth and of Hispanic heritage—UNO Hispanic Advertising + Design, of Minneapolis.

"We specialize 100 percent on targeting the Hispanic/Latino markets in the U.S.," Fitch explains. "There are ad agencies who specialize in translation, but no advertising/design firms, at least in this area." Luis

Fitch and his wife Carolina count among their client list Jostens, Musicland, Cub Foods, Mervin's, MTV Latino, and Target. These companies know what an important market this is for them, he adds. Research, strategies, communications, packaging, promotions—all need special handling for this special market.

Fitch took a circuitous route to opening his niche office. After graduating from college with a bachelor's in fine arts, he went to work for the design firm Fitch, Inc. (no relation) in the Midwest. NAFTA was underway at the time, and trade between Canada, Mexico, and the United States was becoming more open. Luis Fitch took a keen interest in the agreement's potential.

Sensing that there might be new business opportunities waiting for his employer in Mexico, he asked for and received the okay to visit Mexico City on a scouting expedition. While there, he met with the manager of the largest retailer in Mexico, and within a week, an entire team from Fitch, Inc., was on its way to the capital city.

"I ended up being in charge of all creative communications, not because I was the most senior person, but because I was the only person who could speak Spanish," he recalls. "I also understood the client's marketing issues better and was passionate about the marketing needs of the client."

He had learned at Fitch that as a designer, he could handle anything. The technical aspects of his work he could learn. In less than three years with Fitch, Inc., he had worked as an environmental designer, branding designer, translator, design manager. The relationship between the Mexican retailer and Fitch, Inc., was a success. Now, twelve years later, Luis Fitch is doing the same work for himself.

A Side Street

Fitch was comfortable leaving mainstream design work behind because he was very well-grounded in his abilities as a designer and in his roots as a Hispanic person. His niche is not so much a specialty as it is what is true to him.

His advice to other designers who want to explore other cultural avenues of design is to study your roots carefully. If you can go back to where you came from and build from that base, you will develop something much stronger in your work. And roots do not have to be racially based: A male designer raised in a family with six sisters might have special insights into designing for woman. A designer from the inner city could develop a style or methodology that appeals especially to urban kids.

"What clients are looking for today is not just a capable designer, but someone who truly understands their audience—not because of the color of his skin, but because he really understands the customer's subculture," Fitch says.

He cites another example of a friend who is from the Midwest and who uses that for his inspiration. "A lot of people might be embarrassed by their culture, or they are too separate from it. If you can get back to it, you have a specialty you can use," he adds.

Fitch also advises taking one's specialty to where there is not much direct competition. For instance, Los Angeles is saturated with Art Center graduates; Minneapolis has relatively few. UNO Hispanic Advertising + Design is the only firm of its kind in Minneapolis: The Fitch's have talked about moving their office to Los Angeles, New York, or Miami to be closer to centers of Hispanic populations, but in those locales, the agencies are already 20 to 40 percent Hispanic. Instead, they have chosen to stay close to their clients: Ninety-eight percent of the company's clients are within five square miles of his office in Minneapolis; the remaining two percent are out of state.

"If we went to those cities, we would be just another agency. Here, we are the only ones doing this," Fitch explains.

The designer also recommends combining a personal specialty with a professional specialty. In the case of UNO Hispanic Advertising + Design, Luis and Carolina are specialists in the Hispanic market, but they have also become experts in handling retail. Now, they are the recognized experts in Hispanic retail branding design.

That being said, Luis notes, any niche has to fit what the market wants. If no one is asking for packaging in the Hispanic retail market, for instance, it's impossible to wring success from the combination.

Getting Noticed

Ever since he started in business for himself in 1999, Fitch has poured 10 percent of his profits back into self-promotion. It's like paying yourself back, he says. He also does several exhibits of his fine art each year. He believes that as clients get to know him as a person and as an artist, they can relate to his design work better.

Getting media attention hasn't been particularly difficult: When the press needs to speak with someone who is an expert in Hispanic design, its members invariably call Fitch. But he continues to spark media contacts by always making himself available as a speaker who will speak to almost any age of student. All of the children sitting in front of him are potential clients someday.

Finally, find just the right words that cause your business name to pop up first on Web search engines: When Fitch types in "Hispanic design" on Yahoo! now, his firm name is the first one that appears. And he gets plenty of client queries just from this source.

Stay True to What You Do

Just as a designer can see the advantage of a particular niche, so will clients with less than altruistic purposes. Fitch knows that every retailer in the country is after the Hispanic market right now. But his company will not work for clients who are not planning to address the Hispanic market properly.

He explains: "If a potential client tells Hispanic people, '"shop here,'" I want to know what the people are going to get from it. What exactly is this client going to be giving back to the community." Fitch cites Target as an excellent example of a client who is very generous to its various communities.

"My clients interact directly with me," Fitch explains. "The work is very close to my heart." He has had buy-out offers and knows that he could grow his firm to six times its current size without much trouble. But his goal has always been to do what he is good at, and that's being a Hispanic communicator, not an administrator.

"The hours pass away in this office, and I do not notice them. I love this work. It is in my blood."

WIRED/PLUNKETT + KUHR

Reevaluating Success

It feels appropriate to have the story of John Plunkett and Barbara Kuhr, founders of Wired *magazine, as the final one in this book. It is an inspiring tale of a journey the couple could never have anticipated and in many ways, it is symbolic of the trail every designer travels: No one knows exactly what is ahead, but for the artist, every experience has its value.*

This is also a story of designers doing what they truly wanted to do and accepting the sacrifices which that requires. And part of what this couple had to do at several junctures in their careers was sacrifice everything—walk away from careers and homes to start again. And that has made all the difference.

John Plunkett and Barbara Kuhr have resumes that read like a "who's who" of graphic design. They have worked with the top designers in the field of graphic design, created incredibly high profile projects, and founded *Wired* magazine, but they're most pleased with having honored the pair of precepts by which they run their lives.

"We have always based our work decisions on two things," explains Plunkett, a partner in Plunkett + Kuhr. "First, where do you want to live, and second, what kind of work do you want to do?"

In the late Seventies, he was working for Pentagram, occupying a corner of George Nelson's office. Kuhr was working in Seattle. She specialized in signage and interior space planning; he mostly worked on annual reports. Soon, Kuhr was brought on board at Carbone Smolan to do signage for the Museum of Modern Art.

They were gratified with the work they were doing, but reached what Plunkett calls a defining point in their lives when they decided to put their work on hold, put everything they owned into storage, and move to Europe. Friends and colleagues told them that they were throwing their careers away, but the duo enthusiastically left to live in Paris, where they enrolled in intensive French classes.

"The amazing thing about it is that nearly every interesting thing we have done since then has been related to that trip," Plunkett says.

Jogs in the Road

After a few years, their funds ran out, and they returned to the States, having traveled extensively in Europe and become conversant in French. But they came home in a less than conventional manner: They met two Australians who had built a sailboat and who asked the couple to make the ocean crossing from Paris to the Caribbean with them.

"It really got us away from high-tech culture and gave us perspective: The whole world isn't made up of people sitting behind a desk," Plunkett says. Neither he nor Kuhr were sailing experts: In fact, there were many moments during the twenty-eight-day crossing when they sincerely feared for their safety. The experience gave them plenty of time to think about exactly what they wanted from their lives.

Once safely back on dry land, Plunkett and Kuhr went on to Los Angeles, where they worked with Saul Bass and Deborah Sussman on a variety of signage, exhibition, and print projects. Then one day, Ken Carbone called to say that he was looking for graphic designers who spoke French to work with architect I.M. Pei to develop signage for the Louvre.

"Never in a million years would we have been considered for that job if we he hadn't quit our jobs like everyone told us not to," Plunkett says.

This project was to have another lesson as well: Originally envisioned as a five-year process, after only one year, the American team was pulled out, due to budget tightening and French bureaucracy. The designers were not able to execute the work they had already completed, an extremely frustrating experience that left them knowing for certain that they needed to eventually begin working for themselves.

Back in New York again, Plunkett went to work for Designframe and Kuhr joined up with Chermayeff & Geismar. It was now the late 1980s, and Macs were starting to appear in design offices. The technology was imperfect, but both designers could see the potential in the computer as a tool to make people's lives easier. Computers, paired with fax machines, could completely change the way they worked.

Taking Flight

After several years in New York, they had reached their limit of working for other people and decided to open their own office. Burnt out on the stress of the big city, the couple wanted to move to a more rural area, similar to the places where both of them grew up. The new technology would make it possible for them to work remotely.

So in 1990, they began to look for a small town in the West that had a good airport. After Plunkett spent three days in Park City, Utah, on a ski trip, they knew they had found the right place. Three months later, they made the move, put a down payment on an old miner's cabin in serious need of a rehab, and hoped for the best. There was no money for the second month's mortgage, so the pressure was on.

Kuhr began designing exhibits for New York's Carnegie Hall, remotely, and soon the organizers of the Sundance Film Festival caught wind of the fact that there were two very talented designers in town and became a regular client for the next four years.

But another project was already afoot: Just prior to leaving New York, the partners created a color photocopy-prototype of what would eventually become *Wired.* Both Plunkett and Louis Rossetto, a long-time friend they had met in Paris, had a fascination with magazines, which they would buy from the newsstand by the stack, spread them across the floor, and critique them.

"Magazines like *Life, National Geographic, Look, Esquire,* and *Rolling Stone* were important to us growing up in the Fifties and Sixties, but magazines in the Eighties seemed pointless," Plunkett says. "We thought it would be great to create a magazine that people would actually want to read again."

When they met, Rossetto was working on an obscure magazine that focused on machines that did language translation. Little did he know that he was meeting people who would later be interviewed for *Wired.* It was Rossetto who suggested that they start a magazine about computers. Plunkett and Kuhr still saw the computer as a necessary evil, but Rossetto insisted that the technology would become part of the culture itself.

The trio was joined by Rossetto's partner Jane Metcalfe, and they spent the next two years looking for funding for the new magazine. Eventually, they became attached with Nicholas Negroponti, founder of the MIT Media Lab, who brought in seed investors and who agreed to write a regular column. This latter promise gave the publication instant credibility, and the magazine took off.

In its first year, *Wired* was disproportionately influential, Plunkett says, especially considering the fact that its founders were in dire financial straits. Still, they had complete control over the publication's content, which allowed them to do the quality of design they wanted. And as the Internet and computers took off, so did the popularity of the magazine.

Leaving Again

For the next seven years, *Wired* was the darling of the magazine industry. It won countless awards from admirers and equal amounts of scorn from detractors. But then the publication was doing what its creators intended: getting a reaction from people.

The project soon became larger than any of them expected as the World Wide Web took off. As the magazine succeeded, a Web site of equal influence seemed necessary. "But the magazine was a seven-day-a-week job, and the Web site was a fourteen-day-a-week job. After five years, we were 100 percent exhausted," Plunkett recalls.

Everything up until that point was being done on the team's own sweat equity. The decision was made to offer an IPO so as to bring funding into the group. But the business of delivering news of the future has its good and bad sides: They were definitely ahead of the curve when in came to content and design, but most investors had no idea what the product was all about. The IPO failed, and in its fourth year, the magazine was struggling financially.

Eventually, they had to take on investors in 1996, who doubled their money in 1998 by selling to Condé Nast. The founding partners left the company as Condé Nast was coming in the door.

What is Success?

For the past three years, Plunkett says he and Kuhr have been "recovering from whatever the hell happened for the past seven years." They feel lucky to have escaped with their health and have deliberately slowed down their lives. Kuhr continues to do some exhibit work, and the couple has launched into architectural design. Having enjoyed the rehab of their mining-shack-turned-home, they have bought a few more buildings for redesign and have just completed a new home for a San Francisco friend.

Wired will be a hard act to follow, Plunkett says. It was about the most complete control over a product and content that a designer could have had. But with the privilege comes stress and typically, if you're not careful about business details, not much money. Designers have always inhabited an oddball space between art and commerce. Their best work comes through having complete artistic control of a project, but few businesspeople/clients are comfortable giving that away.

The designers who are the most successful are equally talented in business and creative areas. They create situations where it becomes possible for the design to be successful with the client as well as with suppliers such as printers and distributors. It does no good to create a fantastic design that can't be achieved because of real-world budget or printing limitations. At *Wired,* Plunkett and his partners made design decisions that balanced between making an editorial/creative splash and doing good business. They did not have an endless budget or schedule; the trick was to identify all of the possible constraints and work right up to their edges.

What's Important

The value of their earliest lessons has been underlined again. Plunkett and Kuhr are living in a place they love; they encourage the work to come to them, rather than vice versa. They are doing the kinds of work they like, even if it means leaving their original profession behind.

Finally, Plunkett points out the importance of sometimes doing the brave thing rather than the safe thing.

"People have this vague fear that if they quit their jobs, it will be 'the end.' Or if they do quit, they make the mistake of lining up another job right away. But when they do that, they will never run into whatever was out there waiting for them," he says. "There are a million practical reasons why not to quit your job. Everyone listens to their vague fears too much, while they should be tuned into that optimistic little voice that is telling you that there is something better out there."

INDEX

BOOKS FROM ALLWORTH PRESS

AIGA Professional Practices in Graphic Design: The American Institute of Graphic Arts
edited by Tad Crawford (paperback, 6 3/4 × 9 7/8, 320 pages, $24.95)

Business and Legal Forms for Graphic Designers, Revised Edition
by Tad Crawford and Eva Doman Bruck (paperback, 8 1/2 × 11, 240 pages, includes CD-ROM, $24.95)

The Graphic Designer's Guide to Pricing, Estimating, and Budgeting, Revised Edition
by Theo Stephan Williams (paperback, 6 3/4 × 9 7/8, 208 pages, $19.95)

Careers By Design: A Business Guide for Graphic Designers, Third Edition
by Roz Goldfarb (paperback, 6 × 9, 232 pages, $19.95)

Starting Your Career As a Freelance Illustrator or Graphic Designer, Revised Edition
by Michael Fleishman (paperback, 6 × 9, 272 pages, $19.95)

The Elements of Graphic Design
by Alex White (paperback, 6 1/8 × 9 1/4, 160 pages, $24.95)

Licensing Art and Design, Revised Edition
by Caryn R. Leland (paperback, 6 × 9, 128 pages, $16.95)

The Graphic Design Reader
by Steven Heller (paperback with flaps, 5 1/2 × 8 1/2, 320 pages, $19.95)

The Education of a Design Entrepreneur
edited by Steven Heller (paperback, 6 3/4 × 9 7/8, 288 pages, $21.95)

The Education of an E-Designer
edited by Steven Heller (paperback, 6 3/4 × 9 7/8, 352 pages, $21.95)

The Education of a Graphic Designer
edited by Steven Heller (paperback, 6 3/4 × 9 7/8, 288 pages, $18.95)

Design Issues: How Graphic Design Informs Society
edited by DK Holland (paperback, 6 3/4 × 9 7/8, 288 pages, $21.95)

Looking Closer 4: Critical Writings on Graphic Design
edited by Michael Bierut, William Drenttel, and Steven Heller (paperback, 6 3/4 × 9 7/8, 304 pages, $21.95)

Please write to request our free catalog. To order by credit card, call 1-800-491-2808 or send a check or money order to Allworth Press, 10 East 23rd Street, Suite 510, New York, NY 10010. Include $5 for shipping and handling for the first book ordered and $1 for each additional book. Ten dollars plus $1 for each additional book if ordering from Canada. New York State residents must add sales tax.

To see our complete catalog on the World Wide Web, or to order online, you can find us at *www.allworth.com*.